A JOHN CATT PUBLICATION

HACKING THE CURRICULUM

CREATIVE COMPUTING AND THE POWER OF PLAY

Ian Livingstone &
Shahneila Saeed

First Published 2017

by John Catt Educational Ltd,
12 Deben Mill Business Centre, Old Maltings Approach,
Melton, Woodbridge IP12 1BL

Tel: +44 (0) 1394 389850 Fax: +44 (0) 1394 386893
Email: enquiries@johncatt.com
Website: www.johncatt.com

**© 2017 Ian Livingstone
& Shahneila Saeed**

ISBN: 978 1 909717824

Set and designed by John Catt Educational Limited

"While teaching children computer programming is now generally agreed to be beneficial, there has been a tendency to teach computing as a branch of mathematics, with a focus on abstract concepts over practical applications, and rote learning over creative exploration. In this important work, Livingstone and Saeed make the case that, far from being unrigorous, casting coding and computational thinking as a form of play can bring the new National Curriculum in computing to life for all children, not just those who are considered most "academic". With classroom examples drawn from computer gaming and interactive fiction, *Hacking the Curriculum* has something to offer for educators, volunteers and enthusiasts alike."

Eben Upton CBE, co-founder of the Raspberry Pi Foundation

"One of the biggest issues facing teachers looking to embrace the Computing curriculum is that of confidence about coding and Computer science: *Hacking the Curriculum* helps to knock the confidence issue around coding and Computer Science right out of the park. It not only sets the scene for the case for change relating to the Computing curriculum but gives a persuasive argument with great ideas for how it can be built-in rather than bolted-on to the curriculum, particularly in a Primary setting. It is jam-packed full of creative ideas and references to resources that teachers will be able to use in the classroom and is a resource that teachers will be able to turn to time and time again for ideas around coding and creativity in the classroom."

Mark Anderson, @ICTEvangelist, speaker, consultant, blogger, & author

"The authors argue that the new computing curriculum was only the start of what we need to see in schools. They want to see more blending of creative ideas, computational thinking and digital-making skills; urging educators to try out new approaches and resources. This interesting book shares latest thinking on properly harnessing computational thinking, play based learning and game-based learning. *Hacking the Curriculum* is rich with practical activities, including 'unplugged' computing, and there's also a look back at the introduction, context and potential of interactive fiction."

Ty Goddard, Education Foundation

Contents

Introduction, *Ian Livingstone, Shahneila Saeed* 7

Chapter 1 – The Case for Computer Science in Schools,
            Ian Livingstone 11

Chapter 2 – The 3 Cs: Computing, Computational Thinking
            & Creativity, *Shahneila Saeed* 24

Chapter 3 – Creative Computing Pedagogy, *Shahneila Saeed* 51

Chapter 4 – The Power of Play-Based Learning, *Shahneila Saeed* 76

Chapter 5 – Games & Learning, *Shahneila Saeed* 90

Chapter 6 – Interactive Fiction in Education
            Ian Livingstone and Jonathan Green 115

Chapter 7 – Putting it into Action, *Shahneila Saeed* 129

Chapter 8 – Useful Information, *Shahneila Saeed* 159

Introduction

Whenever children say, 'Let's play,' their friends are likely to be very excited by the suggestion, their imaginations lit up by the prospect of fun. It's the first thing all children want to do, and they do it instinctively.

There is no prescribed formula for play. Play is natural. Play in the broadest sense of the word – from simply 'messing around' and having fun, to organised sport, to role-play, to playing with dolls or model cars or building blocks to solving puzzles to playing board games or video games – is important. It allows us to wind down, de-stress and have fun, but it also has deeper and more tangible cognitive benefits. It is not the waste of time as some people would have you believe, but rather, a very worthwhile activity.

No one actually teaches us how to play (unless of course you consider the organised sport and/or games with rules, but more on that later). We simply just do it, and by so doing, we learn. Babies play, and through play and by interacting with the world around them, they make important discoveries, i.e. what is edible and what isn't (although as adults we may not always agree with them!). Older children in the playground will learn a lot about social interaction and how to deal with a range of moral and ethical dilemmas. It's how they instinctively learn. The thing is, we don't actually ever stop learning that way. At least not instinctively. It's just that the education system has a way of stripping play out of children as they get older. Playtime is left for the playground whilst the serious business of 'rigorous' learning dominates the classroom. Unfortunately, 'fun' and 'enjoyment' are not words usually associated in the context of the secondary classroom. Playful learning is for toddlers only, or so we are told.

The complex world of the 21st Century world is being transformed exponentially by technology, requiring multiple solutions to problems, not just one. Yet school is a place where students are required to conform to a set of rules. They have to meet a strict set of success criteria, and if they don't do it in the exact way that various educational bodies expect them to, then they are judged a failure. They become part of the group of 'less able' kids. Schools and teachers are then judged on how well they support these 'less able' kids. School league table performance point scores rate how well schools deal with the diverse range of their pupils, ensuring all have met the strict set of success criteria. Schools then judge their teachers in the same way. Performance management and appraisals demand that teachers reflect on their class results, set targets, and continuously strive to improve their students in the same direction. Teachers' salaries are dependent on this!

However, academics have long since acknowledged that intelligence isn't a linear scale. Students are not 'more' or 'less' able. Intelligences and areas of strengths differ. Those with greater musical intelligence make gifted musicians, and those with greater bodily-kinaesthetic intelligence will likely make gifted athletes or craftsmen. Trying to compare the two on a linear scale simply doesn't work. You can't accurately judge the intelligence level of a musician by seeing how good they are at crafting. No one would expect to do so either.

So if you can't judge everybody by the same metric, why do we do it? Why are schools judged by the same metrics? Why, in our efforts to get everyone to the top of a singular scale, do we then become more stringent in what the education of those children looks like? Is standardised testing really the best way to assess children's abilities? Is the system in fact using children as guinea pigs to assess schools rather than finding a way to better assess children? Relentless standardised testing of the memory merely punishes the imagination, the point emphasised by respected educationalist Sir Ken Robinson, who said:

*"The problem with conformity in education is that
people are not standardised to begin with."*

Many of today's classrooms leave little or no room for creativity or diverse thinking even though creativity and creative problem-solving are considered to be key 21st Century skills. The World Economic Forum concluded that the three most important skills for jobs in the 2020 world of new technologies and new ways of working will be Creativity, Problem-Solving and Critical Thinking. So how are students going to become creative thinkers and problem solvers if we don't allow them to develop these skills in the classroom? Why are education bodies so set on teaching 'rigorous knowledge' in single academic subjects as the one true way for children to learn? Rote learning may be good for literacy and numeracy, but we also have to teach children how to think. The robots are coming, has nobody heard? There's no point in training our children like robots if real robots are going to take their jobs! Repetitive jobs will become automated. Intellectual capital will replace commodity-based capital. Art and science will come together to create new products and services. The Apple corporation is testament to that. The economic value in their smart phones and tablets does not, in the main, come from the plants that manufacture them, but from the intellectual property in their form and function. It should come as no surprise that the design and functionality of the devices, combined with the business model and ease of use of iTunes and the App Store, led Apple to become the most valuable company in the world. If the UK wishes to maintain its position as a 'Creative Nation', it should ensure that school encourages and promotes diverse thinking and creativity.

This book attempts to make the case for play and creativity in the classroom. The two are interlinked. Play helps develop creative skills. More specifically, it examines the ideas around using play to teach creative computing. By harnessing the power of play-based learning in the classroom, teaching can be transformed so that it fires up imaginations and ignites a passion for learning amongst the students. So while the book focuses on computing and teaching the new computing curriculum in England creatively, it is by no means limited to that. The principles within this book apply equally to other curricula and subject areas across the United Kingdom, and indeed the world.

As citizens of the 21st Century digital world, children both require and deserve an authentic education. This book is targeted at educators, whether you're an academic, a head teacher or a classroom practitioner. We hope there will be something of use for everybody. Try out a new idea. It might work, it might not. You might create something even better. There is no way to predict it. But one thing we hope will happen is that you and your students will learn something valuable in the process.

Finally, although this book attempts to equip teachers and school leaders with the practical skills to improve their provision surrounding computing and coding, we realise that it does not cover aspects surrounding online safety for youngsters. We recognise that online safety is an important part of the computing curriculum, and we feel that other books have covered this area comprehensively.

Have fun!

Ian Livingstone and Shahneila Saeed

Chapter 1

The Case for Computer Science in Schools

Our children are surrounded by computers at school and at home. They run their social lives through their mobile devices, immerse themselves in video games and get a top-up dose of ICT in the National Curriculum. You would be forgiven for thinking that computers are the one thing that no modern pupil is missing out on. However, the narrowness by which some children learn about computing risks creating a generation of digital illiterates, and starving some of the UK's most successful industries of the talent they need to thrive.

I've been privileged to work in the UK's world-beating video games industry for over three decades. Videogame development exemplifies the marriage of art and science, requiring a combination of technical expertise and creative flair. The industry relies on a skilled workforce that can adapt to furious rates of technological change. Unfortunately, the education system has not kept up with this change and is not meeting the needs of children who seek careers in the digital and creative industries. Of course not every child will want to become a software engineer, but it will help them if they know how code works in order to become able digital citizens. They need to be in the driving seat of technology, not the passenger seat. In the 21st Century, Digital Literacy is almost as important as literacy and numeracy. The solution is not just to give every child a computer or tablet and think 'job done'. Computers are a tool to enable digital creativity. And computer science is not just about coding. It's a discipline; a broad mix of computational thinking, problem-solving, decision making, intuitive learning, logic, analysis and creative thinking to be used cross-curricula to solve problems in multiple ways. Dutch computer scientist Edsger Dijkstra observed many years ago that:

> *"Computer science is no more about computers*
> *than astronomy is about telescopes."*

Until September 2014, the National Curriculum in English state schools did not require the teaching of computer science, but ICT – a strange hybrid of desktop publishing lessons and Microsoft tutorials. Whilst Word and Excel are useful vocational skills, they are never going to equip anybody with the skills to become a software engineer or digital artist. Computer science is different. It is a vital, analytical discipline, and a system of problem-solving and logical thinking that is as relevant to the modern world as physics, chemistry or biology. ICT is to computer science what reading is to writing. It is the difference between using an application and making one. It is the difference between consumption and creativity. It is the combination of computer programming skills and creativity by which world-changing companies such as Google, Facebook and Twitter were built. Indeed, in a world where computers define so much of how society works, from how we do business to how we enjoy ourselves, computer science should be regarded as 'essential knowledge'. 21st Century children are born digital natives. They should not be slaves to a user interface, totally uninspired, spending too much time learning how to use proprietary software such as PowerPoint. They need to be creators of digital technology as well as consumers of it. They need to be given digital-making skills to enable them to create their own digital content. Education needs to reflect the world around us. A digital economy cannot be built with a nation of digital illiterates.

I must point out that I am not a computer scientist. But what I do know from my experience in the video games industry is the importance of real computer skills – and how hard it is to recruit high-calibre software engineers in the UK. In 2011 former Culture Minister Ed Vaizey tasked Alex Hope and me to write a skills review of the video games and visual effects industries. We worked with Hasan Bakhshi and Juan Mateos-Garcia, two brilliant researchers from NESTA, the innovation foundation which published the review. *Next Gen* detailed a set of 20 recommendations for government, educators and industry, highlighting the vital role that maths, physics, art and computer science will play in ensuring the growth of the UK's digital, creative and hi-tech industries (www.nesta.org.uk/publications/next-gen). The report warned that the poor quality of teaching computing skills in schools was one of the biggest obstacles to industrial growth. This frustration was common to other sectors not usually associated with computing, from financial services to designing a jet propulsion engine. Companies like Rolls Royce and GSK depend on great software engineers as much as games developers and visual effects companies do. Computing is no longer a marginal skill for experts and geeks – it's essential knowledge for competitive, innovative high-tech businesses. It equips children with problem-solving skills for jobs that do not even exist today.

Next Gen's recommendations were both common sense and evidence-based. NESTA conducted seven IPSOS-Mori surveys to gather evidence and data for the report. Teachers were shown to be equally frustrated by the narrowness of ICT. Recommendation 1 in *Next Gen* was to bring computer science into the National Curriculum as an essential discipline. Recommendation 5 was to include art and computer science in the English Baccalaureate. *Next Gen's* recommendations at first fell on deaf ears at the Department for Education (DfE) which was satisfied with the ICT curriculum despite it focusing on digital consumption rather than digital creativity.

Were these recommendations such a hard ask of DfE to implement? It's not as though computing in schools was anything new. In the 1980s, the BBC Micro was the cornerstone of computing in British schools and the Sinclair Spectrum was an affordable computer for programming at home. So what happened in the intervening years? Eric Schmidt, Chairman of Google, said in his 2011 MacTaggart lecture in Edinburgh that the UK was "throwing away your great computer heritage" by failing to teach programming in schools. "I was flabbergasted to learn that today computer science isn't even taught as standard in UK schools," he said. "Your IT curriculum focuses on teaching how to use software, but gives no insight into how it's made." On art and science he said, "Over the past century, the UK has stopped nurturing its polymaths. You need to bring art and science back together." Former Prime Minister David Cameron was obviously listening. Talking on the subject of computer science education a month later in Tech City, London, Mr Cameron said, "I think Eric Schmidt is right ... we're not doing enough to teach the next generation of programmers."

Eric Schmidt's speech had given *Next Gen* legitimacy, and the Ukie-backed Next Gen Skills campaign, in association with major corporations, industry bodies, and learned societies, increased the intensity of lobbying. Our meetings with special advisers at the DfE surprisingly led to policy change more quickly than had been expected.

It was a great day at the 2012 Bett Show when Michael Gove, former Secretary of State for Education, announced the scrapping of the old ICT curriculum and the introduction of the new Computing curriculum. He said it would be written by industry practitioners. We called for 'creativity' to be at the heart of the new curriculum to make it exciting and relevant to students rather than the dry academic science that the DfE was requiring. Despite the recommendations made by some very creative minds on the curriculum committee, the DfE had its way. But at least it was a good starting point. Computing became a mandatory subject in English Primary and Secondary state schools in September 2014, with the rest of the world watching on with a mixture of envy and fascination. Computing in schools could be transformational for the UK at a time when industry is forced to outsource large parts of its computer programming needs offshore. Not being able to hire enough home-grown talent is madness at a time of high youth unemployment. Putting computer science on the National Curriculum will have a powerful effect: it will end the isolation of computers – the defining technological force of the new century – in a strange quasi-vocational educational ghetto, and instead will prepare our pupils for some of the UK's most successful growth industries, especially the digital and creative industries. There is no reason why schools rooted in traditional academic values cannot teach computer programming alongside the teaching of classics. As a discipline, computer science ticks all the right boxes for the knowledge economy and problem-solving in the digital world.

Of course the big ask is: who is going to teach the teachers? But that should not be a reason not to do it. As a nation we can't afford not to do it. There are several organisations available to help, which include Computing at School (CAS), the proactive affiliate organisation of the British Computer Society. CAS has a network of teachers around the country operating as centres of excellence, offering help and best practice to other teachers. There is the pioneering Ukie-delivered Digital Schoolhouse powered by PlayStation® initiative which is now nationwide. Digital Schoolhouse aims to educate, inspire and engage pupils, teachers and school communities with computing using play-based learning and innovative new pedagogies. The programme brings together leading expertise and innovation from industry and academia into the computing classroom. It delivers a unique personalised CPD model for teachers and is proven to effectively increase both teacher confidence and pupils' educational attainment. There is Code Club, a nationwide network of volunteer-led after-school coding clubs for children aged 9-11. There are over 5,000 Code Clubs in the UK serving over 75,000 children every week in the UK – 40% of which are girls. In 2015, Code Club joined forces with the Raspberry Pi Foundation which has sold over 12 million affordable Pi computers, making it the best-selling British computer of all time. There is CoderDojo, the open source, volunteer-led coding club movement which now has 700 clubs in the UK.

There are an incredible amount of online resources which are free. Look up MIT, the Khan Academy, Code.org, Codecademy, Barefoot Computing etc. Last but not least, consider letting the child who knows more about coding than the teacher take charge of a group learning experience with the teacher acting as a facilitator and learning alongside the children. Let them hack their knowledge together using all the resources available to them. Collaboration and teamwork is key. Having informal peer-to-peer learning via coding clubs in schools can be incredibly beneficial to students.

Mark Zuckerberg, the founder of Facebook, was taught Latin at school. However, he was also taught computer science at university, a subject which not only gave him practical skills but provided the intellectual underpinnings of his blockbuster business. Computer Science is a discipline and should be seen as the new Latin as it underpins the digital world in the same way as Latin underpinned the analogue world. Living in a world being transformed by computers and technology, Britain's schoolchildren deserve to be given the right skills and thought processes to succeed.

The case for creativity

Creativity is a core strength of the UK and gives us an edge as a nation. The UK excels at creating original Intellectual Property. Celebrated around the world, UK music, television, film, games, fashion, publishing, theatre, art, design, advertising, crafts and architecture are by-products of a long history of culture – and counter-culture. Modern Britain is an open, multi-cultural society, a rich talent pool where ideas stream from diverse free-thinkers collaborating to create innovative new products and services. However, beyond giving immeasurable pleasure and enjoyment, the creative industries are vital to economic success. They are an important driver of growth. In the UK they provide almost two million jobs and contribute £84.1 billion to the economy – that's £9.6 million an hour. It's also a very dynamic sector, currently growing three times faster than other industry sectors.

But building the next must-have app or multi-million selling video game requires not only programming ability, but also creative flair. There are now over 2 million apps available on smart phones. When the BAFTA-winning videogame Grand Theft Auto V launched in 2013, it generated global revenues in excess of $1 billion in just three days. It was, and still is, the biggest entertainment franchise in any medium. GTA5 was developed in Scotland. It is a great British success story, yet the media headlines at the time focused on the game's notoriety rather than its huge cultural and economic impact. Paradoxically the creative industries are seen by some as second tier businesses run by self-indulgent 'luvvies'. Widget factories they understand, but digital IP, where the assets are intangible, are perceived to be inferior even though their value is very real. Creative ideas are being turned from concept into reality at a rate that was impossible during the analogue age. Distribution has been transformed by the speed of technological change, and an explosion of digital content is today being served to global markets via super high-speed broadband. Digital disruption is everywhere. Opportunity beckons.

Creative ideas, computational thinking and digital-making skills are necessary to build new technologies, products and services. An authentic education for the digital world requires the curriculum to bring the Arts and sciences together to encourage innovation. Arts and sciences should no longer be a question of either/or. It is vital that school is a place where the imagination can run free and creativity flourishes. It was Albert Einstein who said:

"Imagination is more important than knowledge."

and

"Education is not just the learning of facts but
the training of the mind to think."

STEM (Science, Technology, Engineering & Mathematics) subjects are vital, but it is the multi-disciplinary mix of STEM and the Arts (STEAM) that promotes diverse thinking and creativity. Imagination is the key for the 'maker' generation. Imagination helps us dream what might be possible, and maths makes us understand what is possible. Leonardo da Vinci was not only the world's greatest-ever painter, but also an architect, inventor, mathematician and engineer. His genius was born out of curiosity and imagination. Albert Einstein was not only the world's foremost theoretical physicist, but also as an enthusiastic violinist. Creative endeavour benefits everybody. Today's Nobel laureates in the sciences are seventeen times more likely than the average scientist to be an artist, twelve times as likely to be a poet, and four times as likely to be a musician.

The Arts are the catalyst not just for the creative industries, but for all industry, from engineering to automotive to advertising. Creativity is a valuable intangible asset which is difficult to test and difficult to measure. But that is no reason for the Arts to sit outside the EBacc just because they can't be assessed by standardised testing.

Governments are prone to marginalise creative subjects in the curriculum on the grounds that students would be better served concentrating solely on STEM subjects in order to get a 'proper job'. Whilst politicians recognise the value of culture and praise the growing creative economy, it would be a huge mistake if at the same time the EBacc penalised schools that favour good Arts and creative provision. This would seem counter-intuitive to innovation and the design-led knowledge economy of the 21st Century. Stripping creativity out of computing would be missing the point – and the opportunity. Whilst the UK today looks to China for best practice in STEM education, China looks to the UK for best practice in a good Arts education. China is a forward-looking nation with an ambition to move up the value chain from being 'Made in China' to 'Designed in China'. Its plan is to focus more on creating and owning its own intellectual property rather than being used as an outsourcing facility to make products for other nations. Computational thinking and creativity is central to China's future vision, evolving its STEM education into STEAM. It is therefore vital that the UK should not dilute its Arts offering in schools. The Arts should not be seen as just a way to boost performance in STEM subjects, but to have equal status. If a good Arts education benefits everybody, it should count as part of the EBacc, rather than simply being nice to have. And children also need an entrepreneurial mindset as well as creative ideas and digital skills to bring products and services to market. So perhaps the most appropriate acronym for the modern curriculum should be ESTEAM to include Entrepreneurship.

School should be a place where the Arts are practised, especially art itself which has been overtaken by art consumption or art commentary. This shift in art education as the academic University model, driven by the Humanities, has subsumed art practice and replaced it with criticism and contextual studies. How can creative endeavour flourish when commentators are valued more highly than practitioners? Drawing is to art what grammar is to writing or scales and notes are to music – it is a basic building block. Drawing is a fundamental human activity of expression and helps people gain a richer understanding of themselves and their world. It is not just a worthy craft pursuit, but a base for acquiring other skills. Artists do not learn their craft just by writing an essay about the life and times of John Constable. They need know-how as well as knowledge.

To this end, schools should facilitate more vocational studies. Practical hands-on learning will result in a deeper understanding of all subjects. Skills should be seen to be as important as qualifications, and know-how as important as knowledge. Learning-by-doing will add context. Children should be encouraged to be different, and not be punished for making mistakes to encourage risk-taking in later life. Failure should be seen as success work-in-progress. Einstein also said:

"Anyone who has never made a mistake has never tried anything new."

and

"It is the supreme art of the teacher to awaken joy
in creative expression and knowledge."

There is no reason for children to be bored in school. Why can't learning be fun? If we promote creativity, problem-solving, computational thinking, critical thinking and diverse thinking in children, give them a practical Arts education and digital-making skills, and encourage an entrepreneurial mindset, they might better enjoy their education and learn the skills to become job makers not just job seekers.

The case for games-based learning

When you watch children playing games, do you think that, as well as being entertained, they are learning life skills at the same time? Or do you think they are being turned into mindless zombies?

Today, video games are played by hundreds of millions of people around the world. But playing games is not just about entertainment. Games are a compelling non-linear interactive experience that lets the player control the action rather than passively watching somebody else having all the fun on the screen. Once the misunderstood hobby of teenage boys locked away in their bedrooms, games are now played by everybody on their smart phones, both men and women, and young and old. Games have become part of mainstream culture and are socially, culturally and economically important as music and film. And there is a strong case that they could be good for you too. George Bernard Shaw once said:

> *"We don't stop playing because we get old,*
> *we get old because we stop playing."*

His observation was supported by BBC's Horizon programme in 2015. Scientists measured the cognitive activity of old people, gave them an iPad loaded with games to play and sent them away for a month. On their return, MRI brain scans showed a significant increase in their cognitive activity. The conclusion was that perhaps it would be better to give senior citizens a tablet to play on rather than a tablet to swallow to improve their mental abilities.

Frustratingly, the media has been historically tough on games, writing them off as a trivial distraction or worse. In 1859, Scientific American reported, 'Chess is a mere amusement of a very inferior character, which robs the mind of valuable time that might be devoted to nobler acquirement'. In the 1980s, despite the book getting a whole generation of 10-year-olds reading, the press didn't have many good things to say about *The Warlock of Firetop Mountain*, the first in the hugely popular interactive *Fighting Fantasy* gamebook series authored by Steve Jackson and myself. These were books in which YOU the reader became the hero. The reader took control of the story and made the decisions. *Fighting Fantasy* got a whole generation of children reading in the 1980s. Some 20 million copies have sold worldwide which you would think would be seen as a good thing. But because they were *gamebooks*, they were seen as having little educational value, or worse, were seen as harmful.

I recall a magazine article which warned, 'children actually participate through their imaginations'. As if that was a bad thing to do! Parents sent in petitions to Penguin Books calling for *Fighting Fantasy* to be banned. Yet interactive books were later shown to improve literacy by 17% because of the greater engagement children had with non-linear stories than with linear stories. Giving control to the reader is empowering, and children's imaginations went into overdrive as they went on their fantastic adventures of the mind. But when it comes to video games, it's media that goes into overdrive, blaming them for all of society's ills. Good news about games is seldom reported and so the perception of the games industry remains poor. The consequence of negative reporting is that neither parents nor teachers are aware of the positive attributes of playing games. Yet there is strong evidence to suggest that games skills build life skills, and that playing games is actually good for you.

Games resonate with children and are a contextual hub for learning. Playing a game requires problem-solving, decision making, intuitive learning, trial and error, logic, analysis, management, communication, risk-taking, planning, resource management and computational thinking. Games like Minecraft excite the imagination and naturally promote creativity, curiosity, learning, concentration and community. Games give the player continuous assessment and allow failure in a safe environment. Nobody is punished for making a mistake, and players voluntarily want to play again to beat the game with new strategies and tactics. So why not let children enjoy some learning experiences through a medium they understand and enjoy? Why can't learning be fun?

Human beings are playful by nature. We enter this world as babies, interacting with everything around us. We learn intuitively through curiosity, play and trial and error, all key features in games. Games by definition require problem-solving in order to succeed. Humans love solving puzzles which is central to games like Tetris. We love to build and share, the very essence of Minecraft which can be described as digital LEGO with children designing and building wonderful 3D worlds to share with their friends. What child wouldn't want to be an architect after playing Minecraft? Whether it's playing activity games like Wii Sports or Pokemon Go (burning calories at the same time), simulation games like Rollercoaster Tycoon and Sim City, or strategy games like Civilisation, the experience is likely to be enjoyable and beneficial. Think about the cognitive process of what is happening when games are being played. It's a case of hands on, minds on. Interactivity puts the player in control of the action.

Yes, some games do contain violent content. But that is no reason to set public opinion against the entire games industry. Many films contain extreme violent content yet the film industry is not criticised in the same manner. And like films, games have age ratings. Some games are 18-rated. Films and games have ratings for a reason. The media tends to focus its reporting on games that are 18-rated, sometimes without mentioning they are 18-rated. Not surprisingly, parents are worried about their children being exposed to these games. Age ratings should not be ignored. Children should not be allowed to play games that they are not meant play. But to put things into perspective, over 90% of games are family friendly.

Some parents are understandably worried about the amount of time their children spend playing games. Today's children do spend a lot of time on their screens, whether it's games, the web, social networks, music, messaging, or TV. Digitally native children are more likely to choose a screen over traditional toys when indoors. But put them outside, and they are more likely to choose a ball over a screen. Responsible parenting requires monitoring of all media, including games, to ensure children have a balanced life indoors and outdoors.

When children are playing games, hopefully age-appropriate, they could be having so much fun that they might not respond to you as quickly as you'd like. But don't worry; parents had the same concerns when children were equally unresponsive when they discovered the joy of reading books in the 18th Century. Games certainly give context to learning by simulating real world events and environments, so much so that children become immersed in their learning by taking control. The 20th Century sage on the stage by continuing to teach single subjects to the test risks redundancy by YouTube. Teaching practice needs to enter the 21st Century. Robots will replace 30% of manual jobs so there is no point in training children like robots, as they won't be able to compete with the real thing.

British technology entrepreneur Demis Hassabis sold his artificial intelligence company Deep Mind to Google for some $400 million. He said after the sale, "I've always viewed my obsession with playing games as training the mind in multiple facets." Former President of the United States Barack Obama is quoted as saying that games make education relevant for children. He cited the fact that it was Mark Zuckerberg's interest in playing games that led him to learn to code which in turn resulted in the creation of Facebook.

Simulation games are used as a training tool for pilots, surgeons, the armed forces and other professionals. So when you are next flying to some distant destination, think about how your pilot learned to fly.

Would you prefer they learned by reading a book or by using simulation software? Simulation software is effectively a video game. So let's not think our children will turn into zombies when they are playing games. The chances are they are probably learning some useful life skills. Combined with digital-making and entrepreneurial skills, they might go on to become the next global tech giant.

There is undeniable evidence that Creativity and Computing are vital meta skills for the 21st century, and therefore for an authentic, modern curriculum, children need to have the two Cs as well as the three Rs.

Chapter 2

The 3 Cs: Computing, Computational Thinking & Creativity

The replacement of the outdated ICT curriculum was seen as nothing short of a revolution, and headlines such as "Coding at School..." and "Coding – the new Latin" focused almost purely on the increased emphasis on and the formal introduction of programming into the National Curriculum. The result was many teachers being simply terrified at the prospect of having to teach new programmes of study. Primary schools in particular seemed to have the most difficult task, as by their very nature they were the least likely to have specialist subject staff.

However, contrary to what many people may still believe, programming is only one part of the new programmes of study. Computing within this context is being used more as an 'umbrella term' to incorporate the wider aspects of the discipline. The baby definitely hasn't been thrown out with the bathwater!

Understanding the Computing Curriculum

"A high-quality computing education equips pupils to use computational thinking and creativity to understand and change the world."[1]

The highly ambitious computing curriculum places computational thinking and creativity at the heart of the new programmes of study. These two concepts underpin and sit at the heart of the computing curriculum. They add the additional dimension and encourage digital creativity and play-based learning through subject content statements such as:

- [Key Stage 2] design, write and debug programs that accomplish specific goals, including controlling or simulating physical systems; solve problems by decomposing them into smaller parts

- [Key Stage 2] use logical reasoning to explain how some simple algorithms work and to detect and correct errors in algorithms and programs

- [Key Stage 3] understand several key algorithms that reflect computational thinking ...

- [Key Stage 3] undertake creative projects that involve selecting, using, and combining multiple applications ...

- [Key Stage 4] develop their capability, creativity and knowledge in computer science, digital media and information technology

- [Key Stage 4] develop and apply their analytic, problem-solving, design, and computational thinking skills

Learners are encouraged and *required* to develop their computational thinking and creativity skills in each Key Stage. How we go about doing this will be tackled later on, but for now it is important to know that it is there.

---

1. Computing National Curriculum (September 2013): www.gov.uk/government/ publications/national-curriculum-in-england-computing-programmes-of-study/ national-curriculum-in-england-computing-programmes-of-study

The New ~~Programming~~ Computing Curriculum

Aims

The National Curriculum for computing aims to ensure that all pupils:

- can understand and apply the fundamental principles and concepts of computer science, including abstraction, logic, algorithms and data representation

- can analyse problems in computational terms, and have repeated practical experience of writing computer programs in order to solve such problems

- can evaluate and apply information technology, including new or unfamiliar technologies, analytically to solve problems

- are responsible, competent, confident and creative users of information and communication technology

---

Figure 1: The Aims of the National Curriculum for Computing (2013)[2]

One of the biggest talking points of the new curriculum is the focus on programming. Yet, that's the strangest thing: it's not the programming that's the new element, it's all the other aspects of computer science that schools are now required to teach. Programming was always there, it just wasn't that clearly specified, or in many cases that well taught.

The legacy ICT Programmes of Study was divided into different sections focusing on: finding things out; developing ideas and making things happen; exchanging and sharing information; and reviewing, modifying and evaluating work as it progresses. The programming statements sat in the 'developing ideas and making things happen' section and included:

- [Key Stage 1] how to plan and give instructions to make things happen

- [Key Stage 2] how to create, test, improve and refine sequences of instructions to make things happen and to monitor events and respond to them

- [Key Stage 3] how to use ICT to measure, record, respond to and control events by planning, testing and modifying sequences of instructions

---

2. Extracted from the Computing National Curriculum: www.gov.uk/government/ publications/national-curriculum-in-england-computing-programmes-of-study/ national-curriculum-in-england-computing-programmes-of-study

- [Key Stage 4] apply, as appropriate, the concepts and techniques of using ICT to measure, record, respond to, control and automate events

In some instances, teachers fully understood the requirements and delivered engaging lessons where key programming concepts were covered using environments such as Scratch, FlowOl, WinLogo, GameMaker and more. However, in most other cases this portion of the curriculum was glossed over and either not covered, or not covered to a satisfactory standard. Students were being taught mostly a skills-based curriculum which in particular lent itself to focusing primarily on work-based office skills giving less importance to key concepts.

In 2009 Ofsted released a report entitled 'The Importance of ICT' where they evaluated the practice of the ICT teaching at the time and put forward various recommendations. Their findings included:

> *"Most of the teachers observed had good subject knowledge in some aspects of ICT and were confident and competent users of it. This was generally best where schools had audited the training needs of staff systematically and had begun to tackle any gaps. Teachers' subject knowledge was weakest in data logging, manipulating data and programming."*

In primary schools they found:

> *"Too much emphasis is sometimes placed on pupils using ICT to present their work well, at the expense of developing their skills in handling information, programming and modelling data."*

And in secondary schools:

> *"Students' use of logical operators and functions was basic. They lacked understanding and made limited use of macros, scripts and programming principles and structures."*

Further stating that:

> *"Coverage of control, sensors and databases was limited in many of the schools, as was the provision for students to learn the logical thinking necessary to program, write scripts or macros, which was cursory and superficial."*

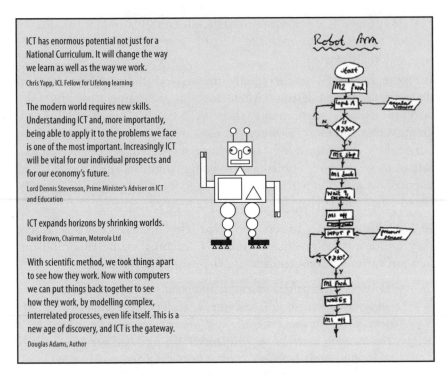

ICT has enormous potential not just for a National Curriculum. It will change the way we learn as well as the way we work.

Chris Yapp, ICL Fellow for Lifelong learning

The modern world requires new skills. Understanding ICT and, more importantly, being able to apply it to the problems we face is one of the most important. Increasingly ICT will be vital for our individual prospects and for our economy's future.

Lord Dennis Stevenson, Prime Minister's Adviser on ICT and Education

ICT expands horizons by shrinking worlds.

David Brown, Chairman, Motorola Ltd

With scientific method, we took things apart to see how they work. Now with computers we can put things back together to see how they work, by modelling complex, interrelated processes, even life itself. This is a new age of discovery, and ICT is the gateway.

Douglas Adams, Author

Figure 2: The Legacy ICT National Curriculum (1999) featured programming.[3]

So, if programming isn't new then what is?

It's the Computer Science that is new. It was important for us to bring the discipline that is Computer Science back onto the curriculum. To raise the status of the subject to be on par with Maths and Science.

As with any discipline Computer Science has underlying principals that generally don't change regardless of the developing technology. In 2012 Computing At School published their suggestions for what these key processes and concepts are in their curriculum document.[4] These include suggestions such as: computation and the language of machines, data and representation, communication and coordination, abstraction

---

3. 1999 ICT National Curriculum, accessed April 2016:
   www.teachfind.com/qcda/ict-subjects-key-stages-1-2-national-curriculum-2
4. Computing At School, Computer Science: A Curriculum for Schools:
   www.computingatschool.org.uk/data/uploads/ComputingCurric.pdf

and design; with key processes including computational thinking and programming.

This document formed the basis of the consultation with the Department for Education when developing the new programmes of study. Therefore, under the new curriculum schools are now required to teach include topics such as: boolean logic, networking principles and data representation alongside computational thinking, programming, digital creativity and e-safety.

The term 'computing' therefore, is an umbrella term that incorporates not just Computer Science but also Digital Literacy and Information Technology, a relationship originally proposed by the Royal Society, in their report 'Shut down or restart'.[5]

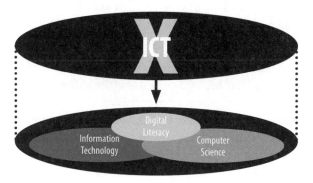

Figure 3: 'Computing' is an umbrella term which includes IT and Digital Literacy alongside Computer Science

The former school curriculum known as ICT has been broken into three distinct disciplines: Information Technology, Digital Literacy and Computer Science. The Royal Society defined computing as "the broad subject area; roughly equivalent to what is called ICT in schools and IT in industry, as the term is generally used". In contrast Computer Science is defined as "The rigorous academic discipline, encompassing programming languages, data structures, algorithms, etc."

---

5. Royal Society, Shut down or restart? A way forward for computing in schools: royalsociety.org/~/media/education/computing-in-schools/2012-01-12-computing-in-schools.pdf

The report elaborates on its definition of Computer Science as a discipline to outline key concepts which include: programming, algorithms, data structures, architecture and communication. More importantly, sitting alongside the concepts are 'methods' or 'ways of thinking' which include: modelling, decomposing problems, generalising algorithms and data and designing, writing, testing and debugging programs. These 'ways of thinking' refer to Computational Thinking techniques which will be described later.

Information Technology in this context should be understood to mean the assembly, deployment, and configuration of digital systems to meet user needs for particular purposes.

A new term that has been defined is Digital Literacy, which is seen as a skill as essential as reading and writing. It isn't thought of as a subject in itself, but then neither are reading and writing. The report outlines its full definition as:

> "...the basic skill or ability to use a computer confidently, safely and
> effectively, including: the ability to use office software such as word
> processors, email and presentation software, the ability to create and
> edit images, audio and video, and the ability to use a web browser
> and internet search engines. These are the skills that teachers of
> other subjects at secondary school should be able to assume that
> their pupils have, as an analogue of being able to read and write."

Understanding creativity

So what is Creativity? It's a prized possession of the human mind. Something we all covet, to be truly creative and inspirational. We want our students to be creative and many of us want to be creative ourselves. But, what is it really? Can we define it, and what does it have to do with computing?

Sir Ken Robinson gave a definition of creativity in his talk at the RSA in 2010.[6] He defines it as the process of having original ideas that have value. He goes on to say that an essential capacity for creativity is divergent thinking

---

6. Ken Robinson (2010), RSA ANIMATE: Changing Education Paradigms,
   youtu.be/zDZFcDGpL4U

which enables us to see and consider lots of possible different answers to a single question, to interpret the actual question in different ways, and to think laterally. A person's capacity for divergent thinking can be tested, and Robinson cites a longitudinal study which tested children and their capacity for divergent thinking. The study showed that while 98% of young children reached 'genius levels' for divergent thinking, as the children grew their levels significantly deteriorated. He puts this deterioration down to education systems of today which can steer children towards seeking a single correct answer independently of any collaboration with their peers, a system which is not reflective of the world of work by any means.

One of the most accepted definitions of creativity was given by notable Cognitive Scientist Margaret Boden (2004) who defined creativity in her book *The Creative Mind: Myths and Mechanisms*[7] as:

> "*Creativity is the ability to come up with ideas or artefacts that are new, surprising, and valuable. 'Ideas,' here, includes concepts, poems, musical compositions, scientific theories, cooking recipes, choreography, jokes ... and so on, and on. 'Artefacts' include paintings, sculpture, steam-engines, vacuum cleaners, pottery, origami, penny-whistles ... and you can name many more.*"

Creative ideas can often seem to be unpredictable, even impossible. Yet they do happen. New ideas are developed all the time. A child in a classroom may become extremely excited by something that they have discovered. This idea is new *to them* but may not be historically new. That doesn't make it any less worthwhile. Encouraging children to make their own discoveries can help generate the excitement and resilience that in turn improves children's educational attainment. Boden (2004) described that as the difference between Psychological Creativity (p-creative) and Historical Creativity (h-creative) where h-creative refers to the fact that not only is the idea new *to you* but *no one else* has ever had that idea before either. H-creative ideas are truly special and what everyone truly appreciates; but for the classroom teacher p-creative ideas are no less valuable. They enable pupil-led learning to take place.

---

7. M. A. Boden, The Creative Mind: Myths and Mechanisms (London: Routledge, 2004). Ebook: books.google.co.uk/books?id=KOR_AgAAQBAJ&lpg=PP1&pg=PR4# v=onepage&q&f=false

Encouraging learners to generate their own ideas and make their own discoveries is a powerful medium in education. Through guided steps, the learners 'discover' computing concepts for themselves; and to them it's something totally new. But they completely understand it, because it's totally their own idea. The role of the teacher then changes, now the teacher's task is to simply provide the vocabulary to enable students to describe their discoveries. If you think back to a traditional classroom that's a huge pedagogical shift.

Consider the traditional 'chalk and talk' lessons, the learning is often very didactic. The teacher gives the vocabulary followed by a definition. Chances are that most learners won't necessarily understand the definition or the purpose of what is being described. They may question the teacher, and the teacher continues to explain. By the end of the lesson you hope that everyone has completely understood not just the term and its definition but also understand the potential implications and applications of it.

"Not having heard something is not as good as having heard it; having heard it is not as good as having seen it; having seen it is not as good as knowing it; knowing it is not as good as putting it into practice." – Xunzi[8]

This widely used quote pretty much sums it up. The original quote (translated above) is thought to be translated from the works of a Chinese Confucian philosopher who lived from 312–230 BC. A shorter version of the quote is widely attributed to Benjamin Franklin: "Tell me and I forget, teach me and I may remember, involve me and I learn." Whoever said it, the essence is the same. Simply 'telling' learners is not enough. Involving them in active learning produces deeper learning and a much better understanding of the concepts covered.

The point is that when learners discover the concepts for themselves, they often do it at a time and pace that suits them. When they make that 'discovery' it's within the context of other things they have learnt or discovered before that. They can 'slot' it in to their mental space. So they instantly understand it and see the purpose behind it. They

---

8. From the John Knoblock translation, which is viewable in Google Books. Accessed March 2016.

understand the 'why' and not just the 'what' it is. For them, the learning and mental leaps from one discovery to another are all part of a natural process. Revert back to the old method and what you have instead is that the teacher is introducing a concept, and some students will grasp it, but some will struggle to fit it into their mental space. They may not be able to contextualise it and therefore will struggle to see its purpose and applications. In other words, they won't understand the 'why'. It also removes ownership of the learning, from them and places it on the teacher. Alternatively, enable learners to make the discoveries themselves and it becomes something that they are proud of, something they have direct ownership of and quite often something they want to continue with.

Problems with pupil engagement, solved? But what if pupils aren't naturally creative? What if they find it difficult to come up with ideas and make their own discoveries? Does that then stifle the process? In her work, Boden goes on to describe three different ways of being creative:

1. Combination – this involves generating new ideas through combining existing ideas and artefacts in ways that we haven't done so before. We use our existing knowledge and often examine it from a different perspective. This type of creativity is one that we are most likely to see in the classroom, with children making their own discoveries of new ideas as they examine what they already know with new ideas that they encounter.

2. Exploration – here we use our structured style of thought, which may be a concept or cultural reference that we are familiar with. We generate new ideas within this space and see possibilities that we hadn't before. Exploration Creativity is something that professional scientists and artists do all the time. They explore their conceptual space to generate new ideas, and enable innovation to happen within their field of expertise.

3. Transformation – this is the most surprising type of creativity as it refers to you thinking of something that you simply couldn't have thought of before. You're changing the way you see the world completely.

So, creativity is diverse and enters virtually every aspect of our lives. It is not something that is limited to artists, musicians, writers etc. Neither is creativity something that you either have or haven't got. It isn't fixed, rather it is something that can be developed over time. Everyone is creative to a certain degree.

Improving your own creative skills. That's quite a powerful concept. It inherently means that this is something that we can nurture and develop amongst our learners. We can teach our students to become more creative over time. Creativity is an aspect of human intelligence that ultimately helps us to adapt. Something that is going to become increasingly important in tomorrow's workforce. Why? Well, most of our students will be entering jobs that haven't been invented yet. In a skills based education system, how can you prepare students for future jobs when you aren't aware of what skills will be required yet? The answer is simple: give students the thinking skills required for them to be able to become resilient learners, adaptable, innovative, imaginative and creative problem solvers. You enable them to identify and teach themselves the skills that they will need.

But if creativity is something that we can teach our students, then what would that teaching look like? Would you have a subject on the curriculum labelled 'Creativity' or would it be something that's mapped across our schemes of work? What do we need to foster creativity? How can we create an environment in our schools and classrooms that enable learners to develop their creative skills?

In order to foster creativity and enable learners to develop their own creative skills, the following criteria are often considered to be important:

- A playful state of mind
- Situations and activities that promote a playful state of mind
- Time and space to let your mind wander and think
- An atmosphere that is free from too much stress
- Ability to bounce ideas off from one another

Under these conditions we can then often begin to see the following develop:[9]

- **Fluency** – to generate quantities of ideas
- **Flexibility** – to create different categories of ideas, and to perceive an idea from different points of view
- **Originality** – to generate new, different, and unique ideas
- **Elaboration** – to expand on an idea

What does that mean and what's the connection with play? Having a 'playful state of mind' is considered important for stimulating learning and creativity. In their report 'The future of play. Defining the role and value of play in the 21st Century', the LEGO Learning Institute stress the importance of time dedicated to free unstructured play as one of the best ways to stimulate learning and creativity. In particular, open and experimental play with little apparent educational content is what works best.

But why? Well, unstructured free play allows your mind to wander, to establish new connections. You are more likely to spark off new ideas by undertaking in free play because you can examine things from a different perspective. Margaret Boden's definitions of Combination and Exploration creativity spring to mind here as perfect examples.

The wandering mind is a powerful factor in promoting creativity. It's the time when our minds are most likely to establish those unique connections. In fact, there is a fair amount of research backing up the idea that sleeping can help you become more creative. Now the suggestion isn't that teachers across the globe suddenly tell their students to start taking naps during lessons. However, there may be something in this. In an article published by BBC Futures[10] discussing the link between sleep and creativity, Stafford describes how dreams allow us to see things in ways that we wouldn't necessarily do so otherwise. In fact, the immediate post sleep, dreamlike state, commonly referred to as Sleep

9. Dr. E. Paul Torrance cited in Jr Imagination, accessed March 2016: www.jrimagination.com/blog/2011/11/11/the-powerful-fours-of-creative-thinking.html
10. Tom Stafford 2013, 'How Sleep Makes you more Creative', accessed March 2016: www.bbc.com/future/story/20131205-how-sleep-makes-you-more-creative

Inertia, is highly valued by many creatives as it allows them to infuse their waking thoughts into the remnants of their dream world. Walker et al (2007) studied the impact of sleep on human relational memory. They found that participants that had a full night's sleep between training and testing were significantly better at resolving the tasks than those who were tested on the same day.

So maybe there is something in this. At the very least, it supports the argument that by encouraging a stress free and playful frame of mind we can help develop our creative abilities. From a teaching point of view, it may not be all that practical to allow your students to let their minds wander all the time. In reality we are bound by schedules and deadlines, we all need our students to have covered a certain number of topics before a particular date. But that doesn't mean that there isn't room for this. It's about achieving a balance; for example, perhaps having a looser lesson structure when beginning a module of work and students are learning and developing new ideas and concepts. We will talk a lot more about pedagogical techniques and play-based learning later in this book, so for now we'll leave that there.

Understanding Computational Thinking (CT)

Computational thinking was a term first coined by Seymour Papert and then much later popularised by Jeannette Wing (2006) and since then has been the subject of several discussions and debates by notable academics.

"Computational thinking builds on the power and limits of computing processes, whether they are executed by a human or by a machine. Computational methods and models give us the courage to solve problems and design systems that no one of us would be capable of tackling alone … Most fundamentally it addresses the question: What is computable? … computational thinking is a fundamental skill for everyone, not just for computer scientists. To reading, writing, and arithmetic, we should add computational thinking to every child's analytical ability."[11]

The emphasis here is on the fact that computational thinking is a thought process. It therefore fits not just the computing curriculum but upon further examination we find that it also underpins most other subjects.

---

11. Wing, J. M. (2006). Wing06-ct, 49(3), 33–35. http://doi.org/10.1145/1118178.1118215

Since 2006, academics such as Professor Paul Curzon[12] from Queen Mary University of London and organisations such as the Computer Science Teachers Association (CSTA)[13], Google[14] and Computing At School (CAS)[15] have published their own definitions of the complete set of computational thinking skills. Generally, everyone tends to agree on the core set of skills; what tends to differ between the authors is the categorisation and classification of those skills within Computational Thinking.

For example, Google have created their Computational Thinking for Educators MOOC[16] which describes the key concepts and helps educators map and use it within their teaching. In their MOOC, Google break down computational thinking into four key areas:

- Decomposition
- Pattern Recognition
- Abstraction
- Algorithm Design

In contrast, CAS (2015) broke computational thinking down into greater detail in their definitive *Computational Thinking: A guide for teachers*. The guide presents computational thinking as a conceptual framework based around lessons learned from previous research. CAS defines the main strands of computational thinking as:

- Logical reasoning
- Algorithmic thinking
- Abstraction
- Decomposition
- Generalisation
- Evaluation

12. www.cs4fn.org/teachers/computationalthinking
13. www.csta.acm.org/Curriculum/sub/CompThinking.html
14. www.google.com/edu/resources/programs/exploring-computational-thinking
15. www.computingatschool.org.uk/computationalthinking
16. computationalthinkingcourse.withgoogle.com

Let's go into these in a little more detail…

Logical reasoning

Logical reasoning enables learners to make sense of problems by analysing existing facts and thinking about these in a clear and logical manner. We often use logical reasoning to make sense of all sorts of things, from the everyday problems that life throws at us to puzzles and games such as Sudoku and Plants Vs Zombies.

In computing we ask our learners to use logical reasoning when they are testing and debugging their programs. We can develop the activity further and ask them to test and debug each other's code. Through logical reasoning we can often employ the other computational thinking techniques such as abstraction, decomposition and algorithmic thinking.

Algorithmic thinking

Algorithmic thinking is arriving at a solution to a problem and the steps necessary to implement it. Another way to think of an algorithm is as a series of instructions or steps to solve a problem. Thought of in this way, we realise that steps to solve problems or instructions can be found all around us, in our everyday lives as well as in other subjects. For example, when following a precise method for a science experiment, or following a recipe for a dish; we use algorithms in maths and even PE teachers will give us the instructions we need to follow when we are learning a new sport.

Good instructions are clear, precise and follow a logical order that leads the person following them to solve the problem. Algorithmic thinking is one of the fundamental thinking skills behind programming. Good programmers are able to think algorithmically. But, described in this way we can see that algorithms can apply to a range of circumstances, not just computer programs.

If we begin to think of algorithms simply as a set of well-defined instructions, we can then begin to develop some interesting and engaging activities around them. Consider the following activity:

Making Faces: Programming with Playdough

Age group

Suitable for all ages

Resources required

- Playdough
- A range of simple images for pupils to recreate using the Playdough. Any images are fine but there is also a great opportunity here for you to bring in some cross-curricular, subject-related images. For example: molecular models in Chemistry, religious symbols for Religious Studies and many more.

What to do

You'll need to divide the class or group into pairs. One partner will become the programmer while the other becomes the 'human computer'. The programmer chooses an image and, ideally, the child acting as the human computer shouldn't be able to see which image has been selected. The programmer now needs to give a set of instructions to the human computer which describe the image. The human computer should attempt to follow these as closely as possible.

You may find that children begin by giving instructions such as, 'take a lump of play dough and shape it into a circle' and 'make two eyes and a smiley face'. While such instructions may appear to be quite specific, they do in fact leave out a lot of detail. If you compare the original image with the resulting model, there is likely to be a significant difference. Children will be able to see this – it's instant feedback on their work. The programmer should be encouraged to change and shape their instructions to try and get the best model. At the end of the activity, it's really beneficial to discuss with the children how long the models took to make and how many different instructions they gave. Ask children to consider whether the same result could have been achieved using a smaller number of instructions. Following this evaluation of their work, encourage children to swap roles within their pairs and to repeat the activity using a new image. Challenge them to try and achieve a more accurate result using fewer instructions.

What the pupils probably won't realise is that what they've been doing is very similar to programming and, at the very least, producing a sequence of instructions. The instant visual feedback provided by the model being produced by their friend will lead to a natural attempt to make improvements, usually in a way quite similar to the testing and debugging that is carried out by programmers.

Actually though, what this activity does is bring some fun into the classroom, and pupils regardless of age will be left giggling. It's a great activity to slip into your lesson before you begin some work on programming as it really sets the context about what good instructions should look like. Preceding your programming based scheme of work with unplugged activities such as this one really helps the concept sink in with the pupils and gets them into the right mindset. The activity encourages problem-solving and requires children to apply other key computational thinking skills such as decomposition, abstraction, generalisation and evaluation.

Download full worksheets and sample images from: www.digitalschoolhouse.org.uk

Computing Programmes of Study Statements covered by this activity:

- 1.1: understand what algorithms are
- 1.2: create and debug simple algorithms
- 1.3: use logical reasoning to predict the behaviour of simple programs
- 2.1: design, write and debug programs that accomplish specific goals
- 2.3: use sequence, selection, and repetition in programs
- 3.1: design, use and evaluate computational abstractions
- 3.2: understand several key algorithms that reflect computational thinking

Refer to Chapter 8 for the fully referenced Computing Programmes of Study

Abstraction

Abstraction is another key thinking skill and often follows on from generalisation. When describing a concept or idea/solution we can make it easier to explain by hiding any unnecessary complexity to reduce the details. Abstraction is yet another key skill that we use in so many ways and in so many subjects. For example, a parent might ask their child "are you ready for school tomorrow?" The child will know that this question includes things like, is the homework done, is the bag ready, is the uniform ready etc. If this is a question that the parent asks regularly they do not need to go into all the details every time. In computing, pupils creating and playing their own computer game would be an abstraction hiding the complexities of the game mechanics underneath.

"Art is the elimination of the unnecessary" – Pablo Picasso.

Abstraction is important as it makes problems easier to think about. There is a skill in it, it's important to choose the right details to hide without losing important information. One popular example is the use of models. Consider a map. A map is a model of a system. That system might be a city, a theme park or the map of the London Underground. If we use the City of London as an example, there are several maps available. You can get a road map of London, as well as the London Underground map, plus special tourist maps. If I was a tourist for a day, a special tourist map would help me plan what attractions I was going to visit today, but I'd use the London Underground map to help me plan how I was going to get from the first attraction to the second. Likewise, the road map may be the best option out of the three if I was planning the route I was going to take while driving from home to my new place of work. Each map is an abstraction of London. They all provide slightly different information; as different details have been hidden. For example, the tourist map may not display all the many small side streets in London; but they are all suitable for purpose.

Being able to understand and use abstractions is a key computational thinking skill and often combines with generalisation and decomposition.

The Guessing Game

Age group
Suitable for all ages

Resources required
- pen and paper
- cards with names of objects or topics printed on them

What to do
This activity will need a little preparation. You will need to either download a pack of cards with names of objects printed on them or create your own. Divide the class into pairs with each pair being given a pack of cards faced down. One person in each pair lifts the top card, reads the word and keeps it secret. Their job now is to draw a representation of that word, and their partner has to guess it as quickly as possible. The quicker the pair completes this the better it is. In fact, this can easily be turned into a class game, with a call to see which pair completes theirs first.

After completing one round of the game, ask the pairs to consider which items of information they ignored and which items they included in their drawings. Jotting these down in their notes helps to solidify their learning here. Discuss why certain items can be ignored and why some items have to be included for the image to be recognisable.

Encourage the pupils to play a few more rounds of the game, after each one considering what was ignored and what was included. End the game with a discussion on how this activity relates to abstraction.

The game can be adapted in various ways. For example, if you made your own guessing cards you could easily give this activity a cross-curricular focus. For example, using names of characters, places or events could easily turn this into an activity that can be used with History, English or Religious Studies.

This activity has been inspired from the CAS Barefoot Resource: barefootcas.org.uk/barefoot-primary-computing-resources/ concepts/abstraction/ks2-introduction-to-abstraction-unplugged-activity/

Computing Programmes of Study Statements covered by this activity:

Abstraction is one of the overarching aims of the computing curriculum which seeks to ensure that all pupils: 'can understand and apply the fundamental principles and concepts of computer science, including abstraction, logic, algorithms and data representation.'

Refer to Chapter 8 for the fully referenced Computing Programmes of Study

Decomposition

Decomposition simply means to break an idea/problem/solution/system down into smaller parts. Each part can then be dealt with (and solved) independently, thereby making larger systems easier to deal with. Pupils constructing products in Design & Technology use this thinking skill all the time. They often have to look at an item (e.g. a chair) and break it down into its smaller parts (e.g. legs, seat, back rest etc.). Each part can then be individually designed and adapted.

Decomposition allows large and complex systems to be developed simultaneously by teams of people. For example, consider popular games such as the Assassins Creed series, Tomb Raider or FIFA. These are large and complex games and are developed over years by teams of people. Decomposition enables the game to be broken down into its component parts, so for example, there will be a group of artists responsible for creating all the in-game artwork, sound engineers, programmers and many more. Each person will have their own set of responsibilities. Yet, when we play the game we see a single product.

Generalisation

Generalisation is looking at the algorithms that we have developed to identify patterns. Can we spot any patterns and find ways to describe them? Doing so would allow us to adapt our algorithm/solution to a wider range of problems. For example, at primary level pupils need to learn about the relationship between shapes and angles. They may start off by drawing a square and studying its internal angles, and then by doing the same for a triangle. Moving on to study hexagons and octagons and the relationship between the internal angles and number of sides of the shape becomes much clearer. We generalise our solutions so that they can also work for other problems.

We can solve new problems quickly if we base them on previous solutions to other similar problems. For example, asking ourselves if the new problem is similar to something that we have already solved or even by considering the differences are important considerations to enable us to generalise effectively. They allow us to recognise the patterns in data and processes, or in our algorithms. Sometimes we will find that a specific algorithm that solved a single problem can be easily adapted to solve an entire set of similar problems. That way whenever a similar problem arises, the general solution can be applied. It makes our work much more effective.

Evaluation

Evaluation is a thinking skill that teachers will already be familiar with. We ask pupils to evaluate the effectiveness of their work all the time. The only thing to remember here is that in computing we are often looking at the effectiveness of algorithms. Does the algorithm do the job it is designed to do? Is it fast enough? Is it fit for purpose? A chef will evaluate their recipe by testing it first. They will follow their recipe to make the dish, and taste it when it's done. At that point they will consider the taste of the dish – do spices need to be added for instance – as well as how long it took to make. They may also consider whether the recipe is easy enough for other chefs to follow without making mistakes. The answers to these questions will help them adapt and further improve their recipe as required.

Pixel Puzzle

Age group
Suitable for all ages

Resources required
Worksheets available to download from:
teachinglondoncomputing.org/pixel-puzzles

What to do
Pixel Puzzles are based on the popular Paint by Numbers activities. An image is broken down into individual pixels, with a number representing the colour. This simple colouring activity can engage young and old alike. You can use the worksheets (available to download online from Teaching London Computing), make your own or even use LEGO bricks instead.

The activity helps the learners gain a deeper understanding of image representation and compression. The puzzles come in various forms from a simple variant of colour-by-numbers to more complex puzzles based on compression where images are represented by fewer numbers so take up less storage – but can you get them back! Each representation needs its own algorithm to follow to get the image back.

The activity helps learners cover the following topics in the National Curriculum:

- algorithms
- representation of images
- pixels and raster graphics
- compression algorithms
- run length encoding
- data representation
- logical thinking
- computational thinking

For primary age students it can support with numeracy, counting, colours and symmetry.

Instructions: Simple colour-by-number puzzles

Each square holds a number that tells you the colour to colour in that square. Look up the colours in the key.

Explore different algorithms for colouring them in. For example:

1. Work along the rows colouring each pixel in turn before moving to the next row.
2. Pick a colour then work along the rows, colouring pixels of only that colour. When you get to the end of the grid, pick the next colour and start again. Repeat this until you run out of colours.
3. Pick an uncoloured square and colour it, then colour all pixels around it that are the same number, moving outwards until their are no more adjacent pixels with

that number. Then pick a new uncoloured square and repeat until the whole picture is done.

This activity has been developed by Queen Mary University of London for the Teaching London Computing initiative which has received support from the Mayor of London.

Computing Programmes of Study Statements covered by this activity:

Computational Thinking including its components is highlighted in the purpose of the programmes of study and is part of the overarching aims of the computing curriculum which seeks to ensure that all pupils: 'can understand and apply the fundamental principles and concepts of computer science, including abstraction, logic, algorithms and data representation.'

- 1.1: understand what algorithms are
- 1.2: create and debug simple algorithms
- 1.3: use logical reasoning to predict the behaviour of simple programs
- 2.1: design, write and debug programs that accomplish specific goals
- 2.2: use sequence, selection, and repetition in programs
- 2.3: use logical reasoning to explain how some simple algorithms work ...
- 3.1: design, use and evaluate computational abstractions
- 3.2: understand several key algorithms that reflect computational thinking
- 3.6: ... understand how data of various types ... can be represented and manipulated digitally ...

Refer to Chapter 8 for the fully referenced Computing Programmes of Study

Rethinking the way we teach programming

Consider your programming lessons.

Do you tell your pupils what code to write? Or do you allow them to work it out for themselves? It is very easy to provide 'too much help'. As a trainee IT teacher my mentors always told me one way to avoid 'doing the work for the child' was to never touch the mouse or keyboard when helping a pupil with their work. That way I had to ensure that I guided and prompted them rather than take over their work. That was a great strategy, except the only issue is that we can often find a way around this (whether we realise it or not). I once observed a lesson where a teacher was using Scratch with a Year 9 class. During the lesson the pupils mostly seemed to be getting on with their work, there hadn't been a demonstration at the beginning and everyone knew what they were doing. The issue arose during the lesson when pupils started to become 'stuck' in the task and found that their program wasn't working. When questioned, the pupils were unable to identify why their program wasn't working, or even what various elements of their code were supposed to do. They were completely unable to pull apart their code and debug their work at all. How did the teacher support them? She pointed them to a word document on a shared drive and asked them to compare their code with the answer shown there in a screenshot. According to this teacher, if their code wasn't working it was purely because they hadn't copied it correctly!

Now there were lots of issues with that lesson, but it is generally better to allow pupils to arrive at their own solutions. They may not all have the answer by the time that you want it, but they will achieve greater ownership over their work, better understanding and resilience. They are more likely to use and develop their computational thinking skills and creativity and over time will develop a deeper understanding and make better progress overall.

When your pupils are programming their solution, do they go straight onto the machines and begin inputting their code? How about asking them to write the steps out first? It doesn't have to be complicated. Their steps could be written out as bullet points, a diagram or drawn out as a storyboard. That's pseudocode! It's great practice, helps them develop their algorithmic thinking skills and allows them to ensure their program is logically correct before it is entered. Thinking through what you want to do before you do it actually makes the programming environment easier to learn. For example, a pupil has been given a task to write a small program in a language that they are still learning. By trying to solve the problem by entering their code directly with very little prior thought means that they are actually doing two things: 1) working out what the steps to the solution should be; and 2) learning the syntax of the programming language that they are learning. That's a huge ask, especially for our younger pupils. By encouraging them to carefully consider the steps of their program before they attempt to code it, you are separating the issues. They work out the logic first and then they deal with the syntax. Dealing with these things one at a time makes both much easier to tackle. Try it in your classroom next time, you'll find that the students are more likely to achieve the desired solution with fewer errors. It also encourages independent thinking.

What if your students shared their answer with their peers? Many teachers do this already, but if you haven't tried it then it's definitely worth doing. Ask your students to write their algorithm down and then swap it with a peer. The pupils then read through each other's algorithm and try to see if it makes sense. At this point because the algorithm is simply written in whatever format the pupil finds comfortable there is no syntax involved and they are able to focus purely on the logical aspects of the program. For example, are the steps in the correct order, will the program produce the results that I want? The pupils can then share their feedback with each other and refine their work. You will find that pupils are able to go through and completely debug and refine their programs before they ever even use a computer! It's a valuable activity that allows them to develop several key computational thinking concepts. For example, algorithmic thinking, evaluation, logical reasoning and decomposition.

When the students finally do make it onto the computer then their job is simply to find the right syntax to match their instructions. This becomes a much easier process, and if followed you'll find that much less teacher intervention is required. If the pupil's instructions are written well enough then they may be able to tinker and use logical reasoning to find the right syntax to match their code. It's a fantastic exercise in developing pupil resilience.

Chapter 3

Creative Computing Pedagogy

"Creativity is intelligence having fun" – Albert Einstein

So creativity is important, it's so important it's in the first sentence of the computing programmes of study. But, isn't creativity something that we have already been encouraging in our old ICT lessons for years now? Why the big deal?

Consider the work we used to ask our learners to undertake. We can all recall the endless PowerPoint slideshows. They ranged from the very simple to some quite complex works of artistic creativity including non-stop animation and interactivity. I personally remember some beautifully constructed 'Find Spot' type interactive stories developed entirely in PowerPoint. But it didn't stop there, we also had endless units of work on desktop publishing with an array of posters being developed on e-safety. Many schools also ventured into graphic and video editing, with some exploring flash animation and more.

Isn't that creative?

Well yes, those topics do have a typically creative nature to them, you'd think that they would allow students to explore their full creative potential. But the reality didn't always match up to the dream.

Think of that graphic editing lesson. The students have a brief. They need to create a new image that is actually a composite of several images with additional filtering options added. Students needed to be taught how to use the software, so there was a lot of teacher led activity using variations of the 'demo and do' approach to show learners how to use various features within the software package. For support some teachers gave help sheets which outline the specific tasks that need to be done to achieve the outcome, with screenshots showing exactly how it should look. The result was often that you ended up with 30 variations of the same image. How much of their own creative flair were the students able to use? Did we just suck the creativity out of the lesson?

Don't get me wrong, there were probably lots of lessons around the country that were simply amazing. However, there were likely to be a lot more lessons that really weren't.

And the truth is, lessons were probably a mixture. But one thing is definite, our teaching style was typically didactic. Almost to the point where when you had enough experience you didn't really need to plan your lessons all that much. You simply needed to decide *what* you were going to teach and then slot that content into your existing lesson structure. The routine was the same, perhaps even something like this:

- Welcome students into the class, settle them down and take the register
- Maybe a starter activity?
- Introduce the topic and learning objectives for the day
- Demonstrate the skills required on the Interactive Whiteboard
- Distribute the resources
- Students continue with task set, seeking help from peers, teacher, and supporting worksheets.
- End the lesson – do a plenary?

Sound familiar?

It was an incredibly useful approach. It saved an awful lot of time for teachers who already had a schedule that was far too full. Planning an innovative and effective lesson that meets the needs of all the learners in the room can be a time consuming activity, several hours can be spent simply preparing for a single hour of teaching. Especially if you are newer to the profession or less confident in the subject content. In an environment where planning lessons is one activity you increasingly have the least amount of time for (especially if you're in middle management), being able to save time by sticking to the same tried and tested pedagogical technique was invaluable.

The traditional pedagogical approach – did it encourage creativity?

Countless papers and reports have criticised the legacy curriculum for its content. We know it didn't work, it simply didn't have the longer term benefits that we had wanted for our students. Many teachers reported feeling as if they were simply 'Microsoft Ambassadors' and GCSE IT wasn't much better. So when a small minority of students ventured onto an A-level Computing course many were completely thrown by the subject content and skills required, it was almost an alien subject, one that they were completely unfamiliar with.

But, many didn't even make it that far. IT was perceived as a non-essential subject that held little if any value.

Going back to our 'creative lessons', while the teachers integrating video, graphic and sound editing in lessons may have felt adventurous and pioneering, the truth was that students were already moving far beyond that in their own homes.

Many more lessons though were far from bearing any resemblance towards any aspect of creativity. The endless football league spreadsheets, disco models, and financial analysis reports written for head teachers provided an uninspiring curriculum; and teaching Year 8s how to do a mail merge definitely didn't help matters. The students were bored and disconnected. The work covered during lessons bore little resemblance to their experience of computing and technology outside of school.

Then there was the clear gender divide. While the boys were more likely to stick with it, the girls steered clear. I'm not sure spending a month of lessons developing a spreadsheet to calculate imaginary football league results helped. Some efforts were made to address this. One popular attempt was the CC4G, Computer Club for Girls. Now known as TechFuture Girls and run by the Tech Partnership, the original model while highly successful in some schools was poorly received by other (typically) co-ed schools. The boys felt offended at being left out, and the girls felt patronised by the idea of the club.

So no, the traditional approach didn't meet the needs of the learners. In fact, as the GCSE, A-level and Undergraduate numbers show, it contributed towards turning the students away. The only exceptions were those schools that made it compulsory for all GCSE students to sit through an ICT qualification at KS4. Those students weren't left with any choice in the matter and often worked towards a vocational qualification rather than the actual GCSE.

Lessons typically left little or no room for creativity due to the very nature of the content and the way it was delivered. Teacher expectations and detailed worksheets that outlined every task in minute detail typically meant that while we felt that our tasks were 'open ended', we still steered our students to completing the work in one particular way. Not much room for students to come up with their own discoveries in either of Boden's three categories (Combination, Exploration, Transformation).

Why do we need to do things differently?

The new curriculum has brought with it a new set of demands in the shape of concepts and skills that we have previously only ever taught to A-level or maybe GCSE Students. With your older students, you can 'chalk and talk' your way through topics such as networking and data representation. Okay, it's not ideal or even anywhere near being best practice, but it's *doable*. Now try doing the same with an 11-year-old, or better yet with a 6-year-old!

Not a pretty picture. The truth is, the traditional way of teaching ICT simply will not work for the new computing curriculum. If we try then we run the risk of turning computing into a dull and uninspiring subject that students do not connect with. We need to engage them and get them involved, enable them to make their own discoveries. But isn't that easier said than done? After all, who has ever delivered these concepts to ones so young before?

I think that's the reason that makes this so exciting. If we are going to get the new curriculum right, we *must experiment* with our methods of delivery. We don't have all the answers yet, but through experimentation, trial and error and research we do have some indications of what works.

Never before has the need to innovate with the curriculum been so great. It's an exciting time to be a computing teacher. Previously, Key Stage 3 in secondary schools ran the risk of becoming the 'forgotten phase', taking second place always to teaching at GCSE and Key Stage 5. Now in many schools across the country it is the hotbed of innovation, with many new exciting developments taking place as a result of practitioner research in the classroom.

From the BBC Micro:Bit going out to every Year 7 student in England to schools developing their own maker labs for students … encouraging them to tinker and make their own creative discoveries is beginning to take off.

Industry interest has also stepped up. The landmark Livingstone-Hope NextGen Skills report was the first to connect what was happening in the classroom directly with the impact on our digital workforce. The publication of the report sparked off a range of outcomes, including the Ukie-funded NextGen skills campaign, NextGen Skills Academy and the pioneering Digital Schoolhouse Programme.

Other organisations have also made huge strides in development. Google have launched their computational thinking course for educators, and Microsoft have added Project Spark and Minecraft to their offer of graphical programming environments to schools as well as Kodu. Likewise, the Apple iTunes App Store and Google Play store are inundated with numerous apps to teach programming and algorithmic thinking.

When talking about 'strides in development' the impact of the Raspberry Pi is a development that simply cannot be ignored. The brainchild of Eben Upton, the Raspberry Pi brought physical computing back into the classroom with a bang. This credit card sized computer, which was as powerful as any average desktop reignited imaginations, and appeared on Christmas wish lists across the country. For £22 you could buy a device which would function like any other computer. Now with the numerous range of ports and slots available you can connect any number of accessories with it. This makes the tiny computer extremely powerful, and its been a huge hit not just with the children but with hobbyists worldwide. Raspberry Pis have been used to do some pretty amazing things, from flying into space to powering a Minecraft based drinks machine.

The work of the Raspberry Pi Foundation doesn't just end with the creation of the device, they've gone one step further and have developed numerous resources to help empower teachers and inspire children. From lesson plans and literature to magazines, events and training programmes. In 2015 they announced their partnership with Code Club and together they aim to reach out to children to help them build their ideas with code.

However, the Raspberry Pi is no longer the only device on the market. More recently the BBC launched their Micro:Bit to every Year 7 student in the country. Intel also have released their Genuino board, and the Crumble device is also gaining momentum with primary age teaching. These recent changes have subsequently seen a rise in ed-tech companies, each bringing a new wave of creative resources into the classroom. Tech Will Save Us, Code Kingdoms, Cannybots and Now>Press>Play are amongst a host of companies that are pioneering in their approach to teach computing differently. Quite often the resources enable teachers to embed cross-curricular links into the work, thereby providing the all-important 'real world' link in the work being undertaken by students.

With the wealth of resources and educational initiatives on offer for schools, testing out new lesson ideas and expanding school provision to incorporate a range of informal learning opportunities should be the norm not the exception. Failure to embrace the changes will seriously disadvantage our students and their impact on tomorrow's digital economy.

Going Unplugged

You don't need to spend thousands of pounds buying new resources in order to become a leading edge school with computing. In fact, you can innovate without spending a penny (well, almost!).

Computer Science Unplugged is a body of work developed first by Tim Bell and Mike Fellows.[17] The idea behind the work is to take complex concepts such as exploring binary numbers, cryptography and patterns and sorting problems, and deliver it in a kinaesthetic way to children. For example, how computers detect errors is demonstrated through a magic trick which illustrates 2D parity checking.

Their principles are simple:

- **no computers are required to deliver the activity** – *this helps to skip barriers of learning and enables pupils to get to the heart of the concept.*

- **real computer science concepts are represented** – *such as algorithms, artificial intelligence, graphics, programming languages and so on.*

- **the activities are kinaesthetic so the pupils learn by doing** – *the activities use a constructivist approach where the teacher uses the scaffolding provided by the activity to ask questions that lead the pupils to discover the knowledge themselves.*

- **the activities are fun** – *they should leave students with a genuine sense of achievement. All activities have a strong sense of story, and problems are presented as part of this. It adds to the element of fun and enhances engagement. Students are more interested in pirates than privacy.*

- **no specialist equipment needed** – *activities can be carried out using supplies you would regularly find in any classroom, such as pens, paper and whiteboard.*

- **they are for everyone** – *the activities are gender neutral and adaptation according to local culture is recommended.*

- **co-operative** – *co-operation, communication and problem-solving is encouraged.*

- **stand-alone activities** – *each activity should be usable independently of each other.*

- **resilient** – *The instructions are usually just one or two rules and*

17. www.csunplugged.org

a goal that can be expressed in a single sentence (e.g. "Each card is either fully visible or not; how can you display exactly 11 dots?", or "We need to get from any house to any other house; what is the smallest number of paving stones that make this possible.").

What first started as a book is now a living document that has been kept in the public domain under a Creative Commons license, and is undergoing continuous improvement, translation and adaptation to make it more suitable for use in education around the world.[18] It has been translated into numerous languages and has inspired educators across the globe with many leading experts now designing and promoting 'unplugged computing' activities.

The beauty of these activities is their very simplicity. You don't need to be a computer science expert to deliver them, and you also don't need to spend hours preparing a multitude of finicky resources or spend thousands of pounds purchasing specialist equipment. By their very nature they are easy to deliver, and easy to understand; young students and older learners, as well as adults, all pick up the concepts easily.

Why do they work? Quite simply, they enable abstract concepts to become visual and tangible. For example, networking, when traditionally delivered, is the topic that secondary/sixth form students tend to struggle with the most. So how on earth do we teach it to primary age children? Well, the reason many pupils find networking so difficult to grasp is because it's a bit of an abstract concept for them so they can find it a little difficult to create a mental representation of the idea in order to be able to understand it.

Imagine describing a network and the concept of packet switching. If you want students to understand how the networking protocols split up and package data and send it across a network only for it to be re-assembled and compiled at the other end, then regardless of the amount of dodgy

18. Bell, T., Rosamond, F., & Casey, N. (2012). Computer Science Unplugged and related projects in math and computer science popularization. In H. L. Bodlaender, R. Downey, F. V Fomin, & D. Marx (Eds.), The Multivariate Algorithmic Revolution and Beyond: Essays Dedicated to Michael R. Fellows on the Occasion of His 60th Birthday (Vol. LNCS 7370, pp. 398–456). Heidelberg: Springer-Verlag, Berlin, Heidelberg. doi:dl.acm.org/citation.cfm?id=2344236

sketches you draw on the whiteboard there is a certain amount of mental imagery and visualisation that is needed by the student. The student has to create an internal representation of what you are describing.

Think about it, networks, routers, hubs, switches, packets, IP, protocols … it's all just a collection of difficult words, isn't it!? The best way to get around this is to firstly remove the constraints provided by the technical terms – focus on the concepts and simplify them. We know it's incredibly helpful for pupils to be able to visualise how a network actually works. So how would we teach the same concept using an unplugged technique?

Take the activity below as an example:

Nifty Networks

Age group
Key Stage 2 upwards

Resources required
Blank A3 sheets of paper
Pens and pencils
Envelopes (A4 or smaller)

What to do
This activity works best as a whole-class activity. That way the children can all take on the role of nodes, or computers, in a network. Begin by asking the class to stand at various locations around the room – the locations should be completely random but they should all be stood at arm's length from each other.

Select approximately four children from the class and set them a challenge separate from the rest. Give the group a message written on A3 paper and challenge them to fit the message into an A4 envelope. Explain that no folding is allowed but that they can use as many envelopes as they need to. This will inevitably result in them tearing up the message and putting each piece into a separate envelope.

Select a child positioned at the other side of the classroom and explain to the group that they need to get the message to the designated person.

The envelopes should be filtered out to the pupils, or nodes, around the classroom. When the envelopes reach their destination, the recipient then has to remove the separate pieces of paper, or data, from the envelopes and assemble it to discover the original message. They will find this tricky to do initially as they won't know what they have received, so trying to find the original order won't be easy.

While the recipient is trying to decipher the message, ask the group that sent the message how they could make it easier for the recipient to piece the message together. Allow the pupils to suggest and try out various solutions and they will inevitably decide that it will be much easier if the envelopes are labelled in order. Repeat the activity using a new message, this time asking the sender to label the envelopes to help the recipient.

What are the concepts taught? Very simply the pupils have just taken some data, split it up and assigned it to packets. Through their own explorations they have just learnt that packets are much better labelled and thereby they begin to learn the basics of packet switching and encapsulation.

When distributing the envelopes, pupils will instantly be able to see that not all envelopes follow the same path, yet they all arrive at the same destination. Ask some of the pupils, or nodes, why they passed an envelope to one pupil rather than another. Some pupils will inevitably tell you that they did so because one pupil already had an envelope in their hand so they simply gave it to another child. Explain that the internet, particularly routers, generally work in the same way and make the same decisions. They don't always select the shortest path, just what will possibly be the most effective or fastest route.

Repeat the activity but this time, instead of having one targeted recipient, designate two pupils. Explain that no instructions are to be called out to the nodes or the recipient, only instructions written on the envelopes can be used. How do the nodes know where to send the envelopes now? Engage the class in discussion and allow them the opportunity to discover that the envelopes need to be addressed with the recipient's name. And, hey presto, they've just discovered IP addressing!

Tips for extending the activity

- Encourage the recipients to send replies so that you have multiple messages in transit at any particular point

- Simulate a server 'crash' by asking a particular student to sit down and not send or receive any data. What happens?

- Get senders and receivers to work in teams of four. Each student represents a different layer of the TCP/IP stack. For example, one student generates the request (application layer), the second student splits the request into different envelopes to form packets (transport layer), the third student addresses the envelopes (network layer) and the final one sends it on its way (link layer). Give each student their role. What do they do when they receive information rather than send it?

- If the packets are being addressed with the student's names (e.g. Anita), then what happens if there are several students with the same name? How do you differentiate it then? Ask the students to explore various options, this acts as a nice lead in to IP addressing.

The great thing about this activity is that the pupils actually discover a lot of the networking concepts themselves. Your role as a teacher is now more to do with formalising their learning and giving them the more technical vocabulary. Key computational thinking concepts have also been covered during this activity. The pupils will have carried out a lot of logical reasoning when solving the problems, representing a network requires a certain level of abstraction, while being able to extend and adapt what they are doing begins to build in some generalisation. Having discussions surrounding what they've done can also help to build in evaluation skills.

Computing Programmes of Study Statements covered by this activity:

- 2.5: understand computer networks including the internet
- 3.5: understand the hardware and software components that make up computer systems, and how they communicate with one another and with other systems

Refer to Chapter 8 for the fully referenced Computing Programmes of Study

Encouraging pupil-led learning

Allowing pupils to make their own creative discoveries puts the power of learning into their hands, giving them ownership over what they learn. That's a powerful factor as the right techniques can completely transform the atmosphere in the classroom.

Consider one example of such a technique...

I was always looking to incorporate new resources and different ideas into lessons; however, one of my first experiences of pupil-led learning came about through necessity rather than by design! I had just returned to teaching from maternity leave and had forgotten a key skill that I was scheduled to teach in an upcoming lesson. It wasn't until I was on my way to the classroom that I suddenly realised I had completely forgotten to teach myself how to complete it. I had no demonstration prepared and there was no time to change the lesson plan – what was I going to do? Unsure how to teach pupils something I didn't know how to do myself, I decided to set my pupils the challenge of trying to figure out the solution for themselves. The children seized the challenge, exchanged ideas and by the end of the lesson they actually did the demo themselves. The looser lesson format meant that they were incredibly excited and engaged – there was a real buzz in the classroom. By the end of the class I had discovered three different ways to do the skill I had originally forgotten!

I decided to try this method with other classes, including pupils of varying abilities. What was really exciting was that for the first time I saw lower-ability students sharing ideas with their higher-ability peers. Not everybody was able to complete the challenge, but everybody learnt something new which they could then share which created a huge boost in self-esteem and increased pupil engagement in the lesson. One of the most heart-warming moments was seeing the beaming smile on students' faces, particularly ones of 'lower ability' who for the first time were sharing and 'teaching' skills they'd picked up to the 'abler' students in the class.

The strategy also worked with the more challenging classes. Under the more traditional method, pupils that are easily distracted, and dare I say bored, would have to sit through a demonstration and explanation lasting at least five minutes. With interruptions and various behaviour management strategies, this five-minute slot could sometimes stretch to 15 minutes. By removing the demonstration and immersing pupils in the challenge immediately, classroom behaviour made an immediate and sustained improvement. For me it was a revelation, I had never seen any other strategy work so well and have such an impact.

The benefits of such strategies are clear; not only do they increase learner engagement within the lesson, they also:

- Can help improve behaviour management for more challenging classes
- Give learners 'ownership' and enable them to make their own creative discoveries
- Help improve the self-esteem of your learners
- Create a 'buzz' in the classroom
- Help develop resilient learners

- Provide opportunities to develop computational thinking skills
- Save teacher planning and preparation time

The last benefit is key, because let's face it teachers are busy people and all too often no matter how exciting the lesson, if it's too complicated to plan and you're short of time then it is likely to be replaced with a quicker and easier solution. The removal of the demonstration and putting the onus on the learners means that as a teacher you no longer have to be the 'fount of all knowledge'. It's okay if you aren't 100% sure of how to use the tech completely; not knowing everything can help us become better facilitators. Learning alongside the pupils is fun too, and can create greater engagement within the lesson.

There are a multitude of techniques that support and encourage pupil-led learning, and several ways the technique described above could be adapted. For example:

- Allow pupils to do the demonstration half way through, at the end of the lesson or at the beginning of the next. This breaks up and changes the structure of the lesson, allowing for more fluidity in how the lesson develops.
- Set each group a different challenge, then use a jigsaw strategy to enable them to teach each other. For example, this would involve the original group breaking up with each member joining another to create a new group made up of representatives from different groups. Each learner within the group is now in a position where they hold expertise over a skill that they have learnt. It is now their responsibility to share this with the remaining members of their new group. The clear benefit of this technique is that each learner begins developing a new skill as a part of a group, they have the collective support of their peers and as such may go beyond the challenge set them. in the second half of the lesson each individual then becomes an expert, responsible for sharing their knowledge with others and likewise learning from their peers. By the end of the lesson everyone has learnt a wealth of new skills that they may not have managed to get through otherwise.

- Set a longer independent learning challenge as homework or as a research project to cover a series of lessons. Platforms such as Codio[19] are web-based IDEs (Integrated Development Environment) and enable the teacher to set a programming challenge in class for the learners to be able to complete at home. Often the issue with setting tasks such as this were ensuring that learners had the technical requirements on their home machines. With web-based IDEs the work is stored in the cloud, and so learners can easily take their work with them wherever they go.

A literature review carried out by CUREE (Centre for the Use of Research and Evidence in Education)[20] found that key benefits of independent learning included:

- Improved academic performance
- Increased motivation and confidence
- Greater student awareness of their limitations and how to manage them
- Enabling teachers to provide differentiated tasks for students
- Fostering social inclusion by countering alienation

This was supported by improved problem-solving strategies, which is a key soft skill that employers look for. Consider the techniques being used: learners are being asked to work collaboratively, share their expertise with their team, they need to demonstrate what they've learnt so they need to communicate effectively and they may lead a demonstration to the entire class which is a great exercise in public speaking. All these strategies help develop the key soft skills that industry is looking for and that schools need to help develop. Recent reports reveal that graduates are most commonly lacking in problem-solving skills, creative thinking and interpersonal skills.[21] The work starts early, by changing our pedagogy we can help to support the development of these skills.

---

19. www.codio.com
20. Meyer et al (2008), accessed June 2016, cited in www.curee.co.uk/files/publication/%5Bsite-timestamp%5D/ Whatisindependentlearningandwhatarethebenefits.pdf
21. Cited in www.bbc.com/capital/story/20151118-this-is-the-real-reason-new-graduates-cant-get-hired

Two heads are better than one

Ask students to individually create their solutions and many of them may make something great; however, ask students to create solutions collaboratively in teams and they are likely to come up with something amazing.

One clear example of this is always the Apps for Good finalists. Apps for Good[22] is an enrichment programme carried out in over 450 schools across the country and each year supports over 22,000 pupils. The programme connects schools with expert volunteers to support the delivery of the programme to pupils. Pupils work in teams to research and design an app for real issues that they care about. Just like professional entrepreneurs the pupils go through all stages of product development, from idea generation to prototyping and developing business models and marketing.

In each of the project examples seen, the pupils create an app prototype that uniquely addresses a chosen issue. On speaking to the pupils concerned it's clear to see that while the germ of the idea may have been put forward by one person, the final outcome was definitely the result of the entire team. In each of these cases the pupils have created something far more complex and refined than they would have been able to do individually.

The same can be seen in other initiatives, such as the Digital Schoolhouse programme. In all cases, team working and collaboration results in pupils creating work that is far more advanced and complex than what they could have created alone.

Self-Organised Learning Environments

In 1999 Professor Sugata Mitra's pioneering "Hole in the Wall" experiments helped bring the potential of self-organised learning to people's attention across the world. Continued research since then has shown time and again that children with access to the internet can learn almost anything by themselves.

A Self-Organised Learning Environment, or SOLE, can exist anywhere there is a computer, internet connection, and students who are ready

---

22. www.appsforgood.org

to learn. Within a SOLE students are given the freedom to learn collaboratively using the internet. An educator poses a Big Question and students form small groups to find an answer.

During a SOLE session students are free to move around and share information or to change groups at any time; towards the end of a session they have the opportunity to share what they learned with the whole group. SOLE sessions are characterised by discovery, sharing, spontaneity and limited teacher intervention.[23]

So how would you build it into your curriculum? Well consider a typical lesson is likely to have the following structure:

- A 5 to 10 minute starter
- 40 minute main activity
- 15 minute plenary

Your lesson structure won't change. In fact if your lesson is in a room where students can access the internet then no other special resources are really needed (Great! Less planning work required). All you need to do is focus each part of your lesson accordingly. For example:

- Give a 5 minute introduction. You might tell a short story, set a creative prompt, set the scene and pose your big question.
- 40 minutes for pupils to investigate the answer. As a facilitator you may ask open questions and offer encouragement but otherwise you should try to remain invisible. In other words, let the kids get on with it!
- 10 to 20 minutes to review the learning. Allow the pupils to feedback on what they have discovered, facilitate a discussion around their answers. Praise them but also encourage them to consider what they would do differently next time.

So, interested in giving it a go? Each SOLE session has a few rules, ones that we can easily apply to our own daily practices if we wanted to.

1. Organise pupils into groups of four
2. Each group has access to only one computer

---

23. www.theschoolinthecloud.org

3. Students can move groups at any time

4. It's okay to share the learning between groups

5. Everyone can move around and talk freely

6. The teacher remains 'invisible' during the investigation

What's the next step? Choose a Big Question to set the problem around. The School in the Cloud has a set of questions of their own that can be used, or alternatively you can create your own. But here are their tips to get started:

- Big Questions don't usually have easy answers. They are often open and difficult and may be unanswerable. Their aim is to encourage deep and long conversations rather than finding easy answers.

- Good Big Questions usually connect multiple subject areas, so are cross-curricular in their nature. For example, it is better to ask "Why are there no animals bigger than the blue whale?" Rather than ask "What is the largest animal in the world?"

- They should encourage research, debate and critical thinking.

- For students who haven't experienced this pedagogical technique before you may want to start with a simple question, and then move to more open questions as their skills improve. Examples of simple questions could include:
  - What is intelligence?
  - How big is the internet?
  - What work will computers take over doing from people in future?

- Big Questions should be thought-provoking and capture the attention of the learner. Some examples include:
  - Can a machine be creative?
  - Who is responsible if a driverless car kills someone?
  - Are computers more intelligent than dogs?
  - Will robots be conscious one day?

- Will it one day be considered murder to switch off a robot?
- Is an invisibility cloak possible?

SOLE captures the imagination of the pupils. In undertaking the research, the pupils will collaborate with each other to form new avenues for investigation and share their learning, team working plays an important part, as does information presentation. No pupil is left behind, and the cross-curricular nature of the question allows you to link multiple disciplines. Pupil engagement increases and it's not hard to see how that would in turn affect and improve pupil educational attainment.

SOLE is just another pedagogical technique that focuses on pupil-led learning as the key. As with other pupil-led learning techniques, it encourages pupils to make their own creative discoveries and then to share them with their peers. Learning is celebrated and the combined knowledge of the class exceeds the progress that would have been made by more traditional pedagogical techniques.

In short, pupil-led learning techniques help support the development of creative thinking, problem-solving, interpersonal and computational thinking skills. All of which are vital skills for pupils to have for the jobs of tomorrow.

Hook, line and ... sinker?

What factors do you consider when you choose resources for your lesson?

Perhaps you think of:

- What do my students need to learn?
- Will my students engage with it?
- How much time can I devote to this topic?
- What are the needs of the students? How will they learn this best?
- What is most readily available?
- How long will the resource take to prepare before the lesson?
- Is it age and context appropriate?
- Does it cover enough of the curriculum?
- How confident do I feel using this resource?

It is nice to believe that factors such as students' needs, course requirements and engagement take the most priority and win, over and above those that perhaps may not engage students very much but are more readily available and simpler to prepare and use. However, the truth is that more often than not your choice in classroom resources may in fact be driven by the demands placed upon your time to be able to prepare and deliver them effectively in your lesson.

Consider the typical teacher that uses Sunday night planning Monday's lessons … it is unlikely that the teacher is going to use a resource for 9am on Monday morning that they haven't used before and needs lots of planning and preparation time. It is much simpler to fall back onto what we know and and allows us more time to meet the demands from our family and friends for our personal attention.

Experimenting with new ideas doesn't just take confidence, it also takes time, which can be difficult to find if it's not a priority. However, constantly evolving and improving our teaching should be a priority. After all, higher levels of pupil engagement will inevitably lead to higher levels of pupil attainment – it's a bit of a no-brainer really.

So, every once in a while, try switching things around. When you spot an interesting resource instead of considering the learning outcomes first, consider: "Is this fun?", "Will my students enjoy it?", "Can I get them to use it in the lesson somehow?" Once you've then considered all those factors, and if the answer is 'yes' then consider "What part of the curriculum can I tap into with this resource?"

You might be out shopping, at a conference, browsing through literature when you spot a 'fun' idea or resource. It's that lightbulb moment. Found a game that makes you laugh? Then try using it. You might not be able to get it right that first time, but through trial and error you'll find a format that works for you.

Some resources may already illustrate a concept or idea perfectly, in which case it can be simply 'lifted' and placed at the right moment within your lesson. However, it is possible that when choosing a resource, the structure works but the 'content' needs to be modified. This may be just replacing key words with words related to your subject content. Take for example games such as 'Three Word Stories' and 'Word Sneak'. Both games were first aired on the Tonight Show as part of a comedic act with celebrities. However, with a minor tweak of the keywords used within the game it suddenly becomes applicable as an activity for almost any subject. One example of this is the set of Computational Word Games resources published by the Digital Schoolhouse.[24] Both games require the pupils to work together in pairs, with each pupil having a card deck of terms that they keep hidden to themselves. In Three Word Stories the pair together tell a story three words at a time that is made up on the spur of the moment. The goal of each pupil is to try and get their partner to say one of their hidden words. The person who gets through all their hidden words first wins. In Word Sneak the pair have a regular conversation and try to slip in their hidden words one at a time. The person who manages to sneak in all their words without being noticed wins the game. The activities are fun and are guaranteed to produce a lot of giggles in the classroom. However, with a clever mix of technical terminology sprinkled with some random words, the games can be a good way to get pupils to think about what each of the terms mean and their application.

Prioritising pupil engagement in your selection of resources brings the 'fun' back into the classroom and helps to develop curious learners who actively engage with the lesson. Consider the following scenario:

> The teacher is preparing to teach a group of Year 7 students their first introductory lesson into computing and programming. The teacher's main objectives for the lesson are for the students to understand what a computer is; that all computers need to be programmed in order to complete a set task; introduce algorithmic thinking and programming.
>
> Prior to the lesson the teacher brings in and sets out on a table a robot such as, Pleo, Cannybot, Probot or one of the many others available. As the students enter the classroom they will see the robot, the teacher herself draws no attention to the robot but the students begin immediately asking questions about it. Some students go up and touch the robot and try to interact with it.

---

24. www.digitalschoolhouse.org.uk/content/playful-computing

The teacher settles the class, having already established an environment where the students are curious about what is coming next. The introduction focuses on what a computer is, and using student suggestions to build up a definition on the board. The teacher then asks students to identify the computers from a list of devices (all computers) which include non-conventional machines with embedded systems including DLR Cameras, washing machines and cars.

Most of the students only pick out the conventional devices, and when asked why, they reason that the similarity is that all computers have display screens of some kind. The teacher then holds up the robot and asks "Where is the display screen on this then?" The teacher moves on to point out the features and functions of the robot in comparison to the definition of computers built up by the students on the board.

The robot is used to emphasise that it will do nothing unless it is told what to do. Later during the lesson, the students carry out the 'human robot' activity. The activity simply selects a volunteer from the class. The volunteer is then directed by their peers to carry out different actions, in doing so the group will need to carefully consider the precision of their instructions.

The class build upon what they have learnt and focus on developing their knowledge of algorithmic thinking by directing a volunteer to different locations and carry out different actions. They learn that it is important for instructions to be precise.

The teacher may not use the robot again during another lesson. However, by simply making it visible to students as they entered the room the teacher has piqued their curiosity. That one simple act caused a powerful shift and transformed the dynamics of the lesson. Think about it, most often lessons are about the teacher demanding the attention of the students so that they can impart knowledge upon them. However, in this lesson the curious addition to the classroom immediately engaged the students. They began the lesson by 'demanding' knowledge from the teacher. The focus of the lesson is now the teacher answering the student's questions and facilitating their learning.

The teacher is in a powerful situation, they have the power to engineer the situation so that students feel they are making their own discoveries and directing their own learning without realising that it is being discovered within the framework and structure set out by the teacher to help them make progress (along a predefined pathway).

In the scenario given, the robot plays the role of a 'gimmick', it's the hook that engages the students with the lesson content. However, it also provides a real world context and scenario, and it's this scenario that can be used to frame the rest of the lesson. For example, in later lessons the students may examine the structure and programming behind the robot that was on display, going on to first read then modify and finally develop their own program for the robotic device. An alternative extension to this would have been if the teacher had bought in a range of non-conventional computing devices that contained embedded systems. The students could examine these devices to consider why they are computers and what their functions are. This could easily precede a series of lessons which examine computer hardware and architecture.

"A high-quality computing education equips pupils to use computational thinking and creativity to understand and change the world. Computing has deep links with mathematics, science, and design and technology, and provides insights into both natural and artificial systems."
Computing Programmes of Study (2013)

Using video games as a hook

If there is one thing that is known to engage children today it is video games. Often it is argued that their passion for video games is at the detriment of wider social interaction, 'healthier activities' such as sport and, many parents would argue, their studies.

But if students are so engaged in games, should we really be dismissing them so completely as an acceptable activity? Why not instead harness a student's interest in video games by utilising it as a valuable classroom tool? History, Science, Geography lessons and more can come alive through using games in the right way. But it's not just the game content and the hook that they provide that is useful, but also the games themselves. Consider what is needed to develop a game: a good narrative, great artwork, a compelling soundtrack, good game design and something to bring it all together. Considered this way, those aspects of a game naturally fall into school subjects such as English, Art, Music and of course Computing. Yes, games require programming to join all the various elements together, but the programming itself is only one part of the game. The game comes alive by having the right music to enhance the mood of the game play, as well as beautiful artwork and fun game features. More complex games require more: understanding physics so that movement of objects can be simulated correctly for example. Collectively you can argue that games bring together STEAM (Science, Technology, Engineering, Art, Mathematics) in a way that few other mediums can. It is their very nature that makes them such a major pedagogical tool.

We'll talk about the various ways games and video games can be used in the classroom in much more detail, later in the book. For now though, suffice it to say that games are an ideal medium to use play-based learning in the classroom to enhance the delivery of your subject.

Enabling learners to develop their creativity isn't just the remit of the 'creative subjects', but is very much at the heart of computing. It is something teachers can easily achieve, not just by the tasks given to the learners but also by the way the students are directed to complete the tasks. Our pedagogy plays a big part in helping to shape and develop our learner's creative skills. With the wrong pedagogy we can restrict any potential for the development of creative ideas, or with the right ideas we can celebrate and enhance our students' existing skills.

By providing real world contexts we can help learners understand how they can use creativity to change the world. Sometimes it can be hard trying to find where these 'real world contexts' can come from. However, the answer is in the second sentence of the National Curriculum. Computing has deep links with other STEM subjects, and we can use these to add real value and meaning to the work we do in computing.

By linking to subjects such as Maths, Science, D&T and Geography, we can design lessons which 'solve' their problems, thereby enabling our learners to see how computing really has transformed the world around us, and continues to do so.

Chapter 4

The Power of
Play-Based Learning

*"Quality education is about three things: the child, the context
in which the learning takes place, and the knowledge and
understanding which the child develops."*
Tina Bruce

Our relationship with games goes back thousands of years. The earliest
recorded board game is Senet, which dates back to Predynastic and
First Dynasty Pharaohs (around 3500 BC). The world's first known
board games were found in Pharaonic tombs with representations of the
game on wall frescoes and hieroglyphics. While rules on how to play
the game itself have not survived, experts have examined the playing
boards and pieces to attempt to work out the rules behind the games. It
is considered to be an early precursor to the popular game we now know
as Backgammon.

Humans play. We've been playing for as long as we have historical
records to prove it. It's part of our very nature, it's how we learn and
develop from birth upwards. We use play for a variety of purposes,

and researchers now agree that play is critical to support our cognitive development. In fact, learning through play (or play-based learning) is now the recognised pedagogical approach used by pre-school and early years teachers and carers across the world.

> *"The main evidence comes from inspectors' direct observations of the way in which children demonstrate the key characteristics of effective learning: playing and exploring, active learning, creating and thinking critically and their evaluation of how practitioners' teaching supports the learning of children of different ages."*
> *Paragraph 154, page 35 of the Ofsted Early Years Inspection Handbook (August 2015)*

Early Years Foundation Stage teachers assess and judge their pupils based on observations and interactions through play. Ofsted also see play as a key evidence indicator of a child's progress.

But beyond the realms of school judgements, play is something that we do naturally. When a child picks up a game or teaches themselves a new skill they do it because it is fun, because they need to develop that skill to continue what they are doing, whether that is skateboarding, chess, tennis or a video game.

So if play is so important, why then do we exclude it so much from our regular education? Think about it, we spend approximately 15 years in education, doing a standard eight hours per day; excluding weekends – this brings the total to 1305 days, which is 43 months. 43 months of our lives to learn as much as we can through organised schooling. For some children that experience can be a nightmare, one that puts them off any form of schooling or education in the future. But it doesn't have to be that way. Isn't it feasible that if we tap into the power of play we can begin to engage so many more children that potentially run the risk of becoming 'school refusers'?

What is play?

The Oxford English Dictionary[25] defines 'play' as "engage in activity for enjoyment and recreation rather than a serious or practical purpose".

---

25. www.oxforddictionaries.com/definition/english/play

However, the LEGO Foundation go further in their report 'The future of play':

> *To play is to engage. When we play, we pick up objects, ideas, or themes and do whatever we want with them. We turn them upside down and we experiment with them. We might arrive at something inspiring and amazing, but that is not necessarily the point. We play anyway – this is play for its own sake. For humans and some animals, play is a vital part of development. What is more often forgotten is that play is not for children alone but is good for all people, young and old alike.*[26]

The key element here is that during play we engage with something. That may be an object, a fictional scenario made with imaginary characters, a sport or video game. Whatever we play with, the essence is that we simply play for fun, for recreation and that in turn has numerous psychological benefits for not just children, but adults too. In fact, research indicates that play is essential.

Children's play enables them to try out different ways of exploring and perceiving the world along with different techniques to deal with problems within a safe context. It is argued that this in turn helps us develop our problem-solving abilities as humans. How? Pellegrini (2009) argued that it is the fact that when we play the focus is on the method rather than producing an outcome. During play we can try out new ideas and behaviours, we can modify different sequences of behaviour and repeat behaviour if we wish. We can do this in a safe environment and without consequence. It is this ability for us to tinker and explore that enables us to develop alternative perceptions of the world.

Tina Bruce is a play and learning expert and in 2005[27] she produced a list which captured the key elements of play. These are:

- It is an active process without a product.
- It is intrinsically motivated.

---

26. Ackerman et al (2010), The Future of Play: Defining the role and value of play in the 21st Century; LEGO Learning Institute. www.legofoundation.com/nl-nl/research-and-learning/foundation-research/the-future-of-play
27. Bruce, T. (2005), 'Play, the universe and everything!', in Moyles, J., ed., The Excellence of Play: Second edition, Maidenhead: Open University Press

- It exerts no external pressure to conform to rules, pressures, goals, tasks or definite direction. It gives the player control.
- It is about possible, alternative worlds, which lift players to their highest levels of functioning. This involves being imaginative, creative, original and innovative.
- It is about participants wallowing in ideas, feelings and relationships. It involves reflecting on and becoming aware of what we know.
- It actively uses previous first-hand experiences, including struggle, manipulation, exploration, discovery and practice.
- It is sustained, and when in full flow, helps us to function in advance of what we can actually do in our real lives.
- During free-flow play we use technical prowess, mastery and competence we have previously developed and so can be in control.
- It can be initiated by a child or an adult.
- It can be solitary.
- It can be in partnerships or groups, with adults and/or children who will be sensitive to each other.
- It is an integrating mechanism, which brings together everything we learn, know, feel and understand.

These have all been summed up by Bruce as:

Free-flow play = Wallow in past experiences + Technical prowess, competence, mastery and control acquired

In other words:

Free-flow play = past experience + skill

If we simply replace the word 'play' with 'learning' then Bruce's list could just as easily summarise what good learning should look like. For example:

1. It is an active process without a product.

2. It is intrinsically motivated.

3. It exerts no external pressure to conform to rules, pressures, goals, tasks or definite direction. It gives the **learner** control.

4. It is about possible, alternative worlds, which lift **learners** to their highest levels of functioning. This involves being imaginative, creative, original and innovative.

5. It is about **learners** wallowing in ideas, feelings and relationships. It involves reflecting on and becoming aware of what we know.

6. It actively uses previous first-hand experiences, including struggle, manipulation, exploration, discovery and practice.

7. It is sustained, and when in full flow, helps us to function in advance of what we can actually do in our real lives.

8. During free-flow **learning** we use technical prowess, mastery and competence we have previously developed and so can be in control.

9. It can be initiated by a child or an adult.

10. It can be solitary.

11. It can be in partnerships or groups, with adults and/or children who will be sensitive to each other.

12. It is an integrating mechanism, which brings together everything we learn, know, feel and understand.

With the exception of the third point (thinking of exams and qualification pressures), the rest are all possible to replicate in a lesson, or more accurately a 'learning experience'. In fact, isn't that what schools and teachers strive to achieve? To make learning intrinsic and sustained to allow our learners to 'achieve their highest levels of functioning'.

If we go with this interpretation then learning is not all that different to 'play'. In fact many researchers would argue that they are synonymous. We learn through play and there is a wealth of research to prove it.

Play is the freedom to explore without defined/immovable/unchangeable goals set in stone.

We play because we want to play; we should learn because we want to learn. Why not combine the two? Learning through play, or play-based learning can help harness the power of play to engage learners with subject content.

Humans have an intrinsic desire to play, children thrive in it; yet adults consistently undervalue its importance. Researchers recognise that play allows children to create and become masters of their own world, it is here that they master new skills, overcome challenges and prepare for the future by practising adult roles. Play helps them develop new competencies and increase their confidence; play helps them to prepare to take on the world.

What if we continued to hold play as an important part of life up until adulthood? What do we lose as adults by not valuing play and engaging in it as regularly and as often as we can? These questions are difficult to answer and even harder to measure, but they are worth considering. As we plan our curriculums to take into account government changes, considering play and its potential long term impact on our learners is a valuable factor to take into account.

How do we play?

Developmental psychologists generally accept that for intellectual, physical and emotional development there are multiple forms of play. Consider the table on the following page, which has had computing-specific examples appended to it.

Basic Form	Detail	Non-Computing Examples	Computing Examples
PHYSICAL PLAY Inc. Gross motor, fine motor, psychomotor	Construction Deconstruction Manipulation Coordination Adventurous Creative movement Sensory exploration Object play	Building blocks Interlocking blocks Musical instruments Climbing Dancing Junk modelling	Physical computing devices such as: Raspberry Pis, Makey Makey, LEGO WeDo 2.0, Crumbles, BBC Micro:Bit, Arduino
INTELLECTUAL PLAY Inc. Linguistic, scientific, symbolic, mathematical, creative	Communication/ explanation Exploration/problem-solving/investigation Representation/pretend/mini-worlds Aesthetics/imagination/fantasy/innovation	Hearing/telling stories Water play/cooking Dolls house/homes Painting/modelling	Programming e.g. graphical, text based Animations Simulations Graphic/video editing
SOCIAL/EMOTIONAL PLAY Inc. Therapeutic, linguistic, repetitious, empathic, self-concept, gaming	Aggression/relaxation/solitude/parallel play Communication/interaction/cooperation Mastery/control Sympathy/sensitivity Roles/emulation/morality Competition/rules	Wood/music Puppets/telephone Pets/other children Home corner Word/number games	Simulated worlds, video games Exploring computer ethics and legislation through play. Simulated play to demonstrate digital communication.

Figure 4: Mapping examples of computing against basic forms of play

Social/Emotional play

There are many games and resources that use a simulated online world which enable learners to explore a variety of concepts and ideas. Minecraft is one such game that allows students to not only create their own worlds, but also to share their worlds with others. The growing phenomenon of Minecraft allows students to explore the boundaries between acceptable and unacceptable behaviour as well as computing concepts. For example, is it okay to destroy a virtual village that your friend spent a week constructing? For adults the answer is obvious, destroying someone else's hard work is not acceptable. However, for students these boundaries are sometimes unclear. Some for example, would never destroy their friend's 3D model that they constructed out of cardboard but wouldn't give it a second thought in Minecraft. Adult guidance and encouragement is needed here to help make informed and reasoned decisions.

Intellectual play

The *simulated* world such as those experienced through video games, animation and such like is a fantasy one where students can explore behaviours safely. It is a *representation of the real world* that they can use to *pretend* play and develop friendships. The digital world helps them develop a new means of *communicating* with their peers and challenges can be set to encourage them to solve problems.

3D Animation

Open source software such as Blender[28] enables students to *create* detailed animations that are either purely fantasy or based on their *representation of the real world*. 3D animations allow students to *tell their stories* through graphics and animation, it enables them to build upon their past experiences and *explore* their views of the future.

Through animation students are able to combine digital creativity with computational thinking and play-based learning. They develop key *problem-solving* and mathematical skills, as well as developing *mastery* in a set of skills that enable them to *tell stories* using visual *representations* of the world. If the animation is adapted for a classroom, then teachers can work with students to give the work a context and thereby use the medium to explore *Social/Emotional* aspects of play such as *emulating* aspects of *morality* and *exploring* potentially *sensitive* issues in a safe environment.

Physical play

Physical computing

There is an incredibly long list of physical computing devices now available, the table above just lists a few of these. However, you can also add to the list the new generation of AI devices designed for use by children, many of which are being released as toys; these include: Sphero, Dash and Dot, Probot, Cannybots and many more.

---

28. www.blender.org

All these devices allow the students to *construct* and *deconstruct* systems and circuits, enabling students to *manipulate* several *objects* and *coordinate* how they work together to *solve problems*. A robot can be programmed to compete in a race against other robots on a race track that the student has *designed*, to save the prince from the burning castle, or even gather all the red LEGO bricks together into one pile. For students the possibilities are endless.

The same is true with the physical computing devices such as the Raspberry Pis, Crumbles and Makey Makey Devices. With *creativity* and *imagination* students are able to use these devices to convert stairs into a piano, make your t-shirt light up, turn a cardboard box into an interactive monster that responds to light, sound and touch or anything else that they can think of.

Unplugged computing

Unplugged computing activities enable learners to explore computing concepts without the use of digital devices. They tap into the power of play. Consider for example the CS4FN '20-Questions' activity which teaches learners about search algorithms through playing the game. The Digital Schoolhouse 'Making Faces' activity encourages learners to play with playdough to help learn about algorithmic thinking and Barefoot Computing has a range of games and resources to achieve the same aims. Likewise the Institute of Play in the US has a whole body of work which aims to teach a range of subject concepts through games and play.

Play, creativity and computing

"Abstract thinking is a level of thinking about things that is removed from the facts of the 'here and now', and from specific examples of the things or concepts being thought about. Abstract thinkers are able to reflect on events and ideas, and on attributes and relationships separate from the objects that have those attributes or share those relationships."[29]

In order to understand the link between play, creativity and computational thinking it is important to first take a brief look at our own cognitive development. Famous developmental psychologist Jean Piaget put

---

29. www.projectlearnet.org/tutorials/concrete_vs_abstract_thinking.html

forward his theory of cognitive development in children which has been widely accepted by experts. He proposed that children have four stages of thought development. These were:

1. The Sensorimotor Stage (birth to 2 years) – the main development during this stage is to know that an object still continues to exist even if it is hidden.

2. The Preoperational Stage (2 to 7 years) – here, children are able to begin thinking symbolically and understanding that a word or object can represent something other than itself. Although children will continue to have difficulty taking the viewpoint of others.

3. The Concrete Operational Stage (7 to 11 years) – the concrete stage marks the beginning of logical or operational thought, it means they can begin to work things out internally.

4. The Formal Operational Stage (11 years plus) – this stage lasts to adulthood. During this time people develop the ability for abstract thinking, being able to consider abstract concepts and logically test hypotheses.

Essentially, people develop abstract thought over time, it is not a skill that we are born with. Play helps us develop cognitively and over time move from concrete to abstract thinking. So for example, when an adult wants to solve a problem, write a story or reflect on an experience they are able to represent the challenge mentally and consider it from different angles. Children by their very nature are not as easily capable of abstract thought, and they will require the support of real situations and objects to work through the ideas using play as the mechanism.

We can apply the same idea to learning. If we consider the psychological development of children it once again supports the idea that children learn best by doing, by actively exploring and making their own discoveries. Piaget suggested that the assimilation and accommodation of new knowledge required an active learner because problem-solving skills cannot be taught, they must be discovered.

This reinforces everything that we have considered thus far about teaching computing and computational thinking. Play is used by children to naturally develop these skills; this in turn also supports the development of creative skills and abstract thought. Learning how to solve problems is a natural part of human development, so it could be argued that we all carry out computational thinking naturally and develop it in our early years through play. Working with this theme in schools as children get older seems like a natural continuation of what children already do.

So why don't we all do it? With the pressures placed upon schools to achieve high results in examinations, it's all too easy to focus on academic achievement as a pure assimilation of subject content. Then when you factor in the pressures placed upon the time given to deliver subject content, teachers find that they have a lot to cover in not enough time. Under those circumstances it is then all too easy to slip into purely didactic teaching. However, it could be argued that there is always time for a little creative teaching; it can save time, increase learner engagement and confidence, improve a range of thinking skills including computational thinking which in turn should significantly help improve a educational attainment. Here are some tips to help you get started:

1. Learning should be student centred with the teacher facilitating the learning rather than constant direct tuition.

2. The journey students go through and the thought processes involved in writing a computer program are much more important (and provide more valuable information about their knowledge, understanding and progress) than the final lines of code they may print out and hand in for marking.

3. Use active methods that require students to 'discover' or reconstruct ideas and thereby understand the subject content.

4. Use collaborative as well as individual activities. Children can learn a lot from each other.

5. Devise situations that present useful problems, place them within a context so that students can relate to them. 'Why' the students are carrying out an activity is much more important and engaging than 'what' you are actually expecting them to do.

6. Set ongoing challenges that require the students to reconsider their strategy and approach.

7. Evaluate the level of each child's cognitive development so that suitable tasks can be set.

However, many researchers don't completely agree with Piaget. In fact some studies have shown that progressing to the 'formal operational stage' (where abstract thinking develops) is not guaranteed, with some research suggesting that only one-third of adults ever reach the formal operational stage.

Simultaneously, several studies and reports show that as we get older we are less likely to continue to 'play', and if we do then the nature of our play often changes. Play for many adults is an activity engaged in by children. Yet, while we may play differently as adults doing so has clear benefits. Play enables us to see things from a different angle and add a fresh perspective on things. It's a way of developing new ideas. It's no coincidence that many of the world's most successful inventors have had a reputation for being playful. There's a reason behind why companies such as Google are famous for their quirky office features. Adding the sense of 'fun' and play makes our work more enjoyable, loosens our inhibitions and enables our creativity to flow and innovation to take place.

Perhaps if more education was to follow suit with teachers harnessing the power of play in the classroom, then not only would we raise pupil achievement but we would also encourage more students to adopt the philosophy of lifelong learning as a natural part of life.

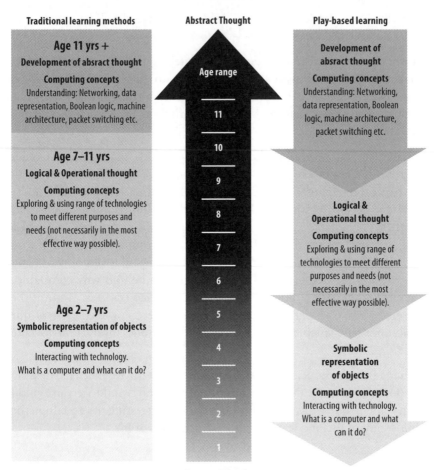

Using play to make abstract concepts more concrete and thereby accessible to younger learners

Traditional learning methods

Age 11 yrs +
Development of absract thought
Computing concepts
Understanding: Networking, data representation, Boolean logic, machine architecture, packet switching etc.

Age 7–11 yrs
Logical & Operational thought
Computing concepts
Exploring & using range of technologies to meet different purposes and needs (not necessarily in the most effective way possible).

Age 2–7 yrs
Symbolic representation of objects
Computing concepts
Interacting with technology. What is a computer and what can it do?

Abstract Thought

Age range

11
10
9
8
7
6
5
4
3
2
1

Concrete Thought

Play-based learning

Development of absract thought
Computing concepts
Understanding: Networking, data representation, Boolean logic, machine architecture, packet switching etc.

Logical & Operational thought
Computing concepts
Exploring & using range of technologies to meet different purposes and needs (not necessarily in the most effective way possible).

Symbolic representation of objects
Computing concepts
Interacting with technology. What is a computer and what can it do?

If we consider where some of the key computing concepts and behaviours sit along Piaget's development of thought, then it's clear to see that the 'tough' concepts such as understanding how networks operate and data representation require some element of abstract thought in order to be able to visualise and understand them. That is, if these concepts are taught using traditional techniques. However, we have already discussed how the power of play can make otherwise abstract concepts more visual and tangible. They make the concepts accessible for those learners that aren't able to create a mental representation of the concept you are trying to describe.

Using the image as a guide it's also easy to see why some learners struggle to achieve or understand computing. We are not teaching them in a learning style that suits them. We already discussed how abstract thought doesn't develop for everyone, or even within similar years for everyone. Different people will be at their own stages of development for this. We already know this as teachers: we are used to differentiating our lesson delivery in order to meet the needs of all the learners in the room. The argument here is simply this: use play to make your differentiation easier. You are much more likely to engage all your learners and support their progress within the subject.

Chapter 5

Games & Learning

Play and games can often seem synonymous, and when we think of games most of us begin thinking of video games. With video games being more popular than ever before, they continue to capture the imaginations of adults and children alike. Increasingly immersive experiences are enhanced by the newer technologies such as Virtual and Augmented Reality. The UK was the 6th largest video game market in 2015 in the world. 99% of 8 to 15-year-olds play games, and 43% of those are girls. Children like playing games. But they don't just like playing them, they want to make them too. The 2015 Young Digital Makers Report by Nesta highlighted that over 55% of young people are already making their own games, and a further 33% would like to make games. With such high numbers of children and young people interested in video games, they simply cannot be ignored by educationalists.

Many teachers who try to innovate in their classrooms have attempted some sort of cross over with video games. Whether that's using video games in lessons or using game mechanics to 'gamify' the classroom, dozens of techniques have been tried and tested by teachers across the world. Increased motivation and pupil engagement is probably one of the most commonly reported outcomes of such work. However, in recent reporting and literature some of the terminology can become confusing as terms are used interchangeably. Perrotta et al (2013)[30] carried out a literature review and put forward three definitions for game-based learning in education. They suggest that:

Game-Based Learning refers to the use of video games to support teaching and learning.

Gamification is a much newer concept than game-based learning. It is about using 'elements' derived from video game design, which are then deployed in a variety of contexts, rather than about using individual video games.

Gameplay is the treatment of topics and ideas as rules, actions, decisions and consequences, rather than as content to be communicated or assimilated. Video games can be seen to allow learners to engage with topics and ideas through interaction and simulation, rather than through the conventional materials and formats of schooling: textbooks, lessons, assignments and so forth.

They went on to find that the use of games in education had a significant positive impact on problem-solving skills, knowledge acquisition, motivation and engagement. The report goes on to make the following recommendations for teachers:

- The evidence suggests that game-based learning can improve engagement and motivation. However, there is still a lot more we don't know about the impact of video games on learning.
- The best way of integrating gaming into teaching is by using it within a clear pedagogic process. In particular:
  - Place learning activities and academic content within the video game's fictional and entertainment context, maintaining a balance between fun and learning.
  - Make the academic content integral to the game rather than an add-on. Content-specific tasks work better when embedded in the fictional context and rules ('mechanics') of the game.

30. Perrotta, C., Featherstone, G., Aston, H. and Houghton, E. (2013). Game-based Learning: Latest Evidence and Future Directions (NFER Research Programme: Innovation in Education). Slough: NFER.

- Carefully plan the roles that you and your learners will take on in the game. Teachers should play roles that allow them to mediate the experience for learners: providing guidance when needed; ensuring that rules are followed; and maintaining a respectful atmosphere.

- Don't try to divorce decontextualised components of a game (such as badges, scores or leaderboards) from the fictional context and rules of the game (the 'mechanics').

Why use games in the classroom?

The reasons given here apply equally in most cases to games in their broadest sense. That is, card and board games as well as the video games we may typically consider. Card and board games are equally engaging and can be used to illustrate a number of computing concepts brilliantly.

- Children play games at home all the time. By using games in our lessons we are more likely to encourage continued learning beyond the classroom.

- Research shows that using games in the classroom increases learner motivation and engagement. Games are fun, and if the learners are having a good time they will want to carry on doing it.

- Developmental psychologists and EYFS teachers recognise the power of learning through play. It's time we tapped into it for older learners.

- Play can make abstract concepts more concrete, thereby making them easier to understand for younger learners. For example, teaching learners how a computer processes instructions can seem like a 'dull' topic and one that they find difficult to visualise. However, turning the concept into a physical activity, such as role play, makes the concept more tangible, and one they can manipulate to make their own discoveries about how computers will need to work in order to operate efficiently. Games and play make otherwise tough concepts accessible to all learners.

- Almost all learners have access to some form of technology that enables gameplay. By using games, we are tapping into their use of the technology.

- Games make differentiation in the classroom easier. A player progresses through the game with increasingly difficult levels, so theoretically faster learners can progress at a faster rate. Likewise, some purpose built games will adapt the next stage of the game depending on player progress made. So everyone gets to play the game at a level that appropriately challenges them. Achieving the same level of differentiation through worksheets can be a bit of a nightmare.

- Purpose built educational games usually have some marking/ scoring system built in – so that saves time spent manually marking 32 exercise books!

- Children learn by doing. Any teacher knows that when the learners have had the opportunity to undertake activities which reinforce the concepts being taught then they are more likely to retain that knowledge in the future. Play-based learning can help put the concepts into practice as well as making them more visual.

- Play-based learning enables student-led learning to take place which in turn can help reinforce the development of computational thinking through the use of techniques such as: reflecting, coding, designing, analysing and applying.[31]

- Games can support collaborative group work between peers. More often than not, people in industry work in teams. Games are usually developed by a group of people for example, with each focusing on their areas of expertise (e.g. it is highly likely that the person responsible for the artwork will not be the same as the programmer for the game). Being able to work in a group, where you effectively tap into the strengths of your team, is a key soft skill required for employment. A lot of play-based learning activities require learners to collaborate with each other, and do so effectively.

---

31. computingatschool.org.uk/computationalthinking

- Most games will help develop problem-solving and logical reasoning skills, which are key aspects of computational thinking.

The power of video games

> *"Through good games design we can leverage deeper and deeper learning as a form of pleasure in people's everyday lives, without any hint of school or schooling...one way (not the only way) to deliver good learning in schools and workplaces would, indeed, be via games or game-like technologies, though we have to be careful not to co-opt young people's cultures for our own purposes." Gee (2007)*[32]

Good video games engage players with powerful forms of learning. In fact one could argue that games are a form of learning that we should make every attempt to capitalise on in schools. Gee (2007) describes the following reasons:

- **Good video games offer players strong identities**. Learning a new domain, whether physics or furniture making, requires learning to see and value work and the world in new ways, in the ways that physicists or furniture-makers would do. Video games allow players learn to view the virtual world through a distinctive identity.

- **They make players think like scientists**. Gee argues that gameplay is built on a cycle of 'hypothesize, probe the world, get a reaction, reflect on the results and then probe again', which is not too dissimilar from experimental science.

- **They let players be producers and not just consumers**. Open ended games can give each player a different experience. Players co-design the game through their actions and decisions. A newer form of games are Sandbox games which give players the tools to develop their own unique experiences within the worlds.

- **They lower the consequences of failure**. When players fail they can pick up from their last save. Players are encouraged to take risks, explore and try new things.

---

32. Gee, J. P. 2007. What Video Games have to teach us about Learning and Literacy. Palgrave Macmillan.

- **They allow players to customise the game to fit their learning and playing styles**. Games will have different difficulty levels, and good games often allow problems to be solved in different ways.

- **All these features enable players to feel a sense of ownership and control; it's their game**.

Good games remain appropriately challenging. They give players a set of challenging problems and then let them practise until they have mastered a set of solutions. Once that's done they then raise the bar and throw another set of problems at the player, ones that may require the player to rethink their previously acquired skills and strategies. Over time players will consolidate the new set of skills and then be given yet a greater challenge. This cycle of consolidating learning and then being appropriately challenged again is something we aim for in schools, classrooms and other learning environments.

In fact, you could map computational thinking onto that previous description if you wanted to. Taking that further, we can argue that games support the delivery of computational thinking. We use computational thinking techniques all the time.

Computational Thinking and video games

Most games (not just traditional educational games) involve some element of problem-solving which requires the player to develop new skills and master new strategies. When new challenges are presented and the player has to rethink their strategy there is an element of evaluation taking place where the player may revise and refine their previous algorithm or strategy for solving the given problem.

In fact if we begin to consider typical gameplay behaviours and features within games and compare them against computational thinking, you find that you can easily map one against the other. The following image map is an attempt to do just that. It is by no means comprehensive and there will be examples that are not on the map; however, it does clearly highlight the similarities. It supports the hypothesis that we can use the medium of games to help develop computational thinking.

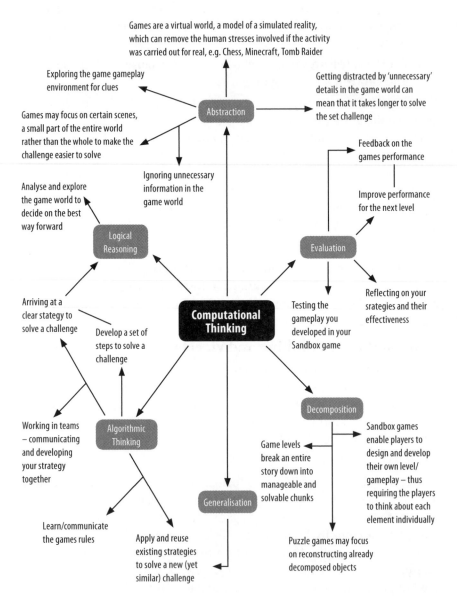

Games are a virtual world, a model of a simulated reality, which can remove the human stresses involved if the activity was carried out for real, e.g. Chess, Minecraft, Tomb Raider

Exploring the game gameplay environment for clues

Getting distracted by 'unnecessary' details in the game world can mean that it takes longer to solve the set challenge

Games may focus on certain scenes, a small part of the entire world rather than the whole to make the challenge easier to solve

Abstraction

Feedback on the games performance

Improve performance for the next level

Analyse and explore the game world to decide on the best way forward

Ignoring unnecessary information in the game world

Logical Reasoning

Evaluation

Reflecting on your strategies and their effectiveness

Arriving at a clear strategy to solve a challenge

Computational Thinking

Testing the gameplay you developed in your Sandbox game

Develop a set of steps to solve a challenge

Working in teams – communicating and developing your strategy together

Decomposition

Sandbox games enable players to design and develop their own level/ gameplay – thus requiring the players to think about each element individually

Algorithmic Thinking

Game levels break an entire story down into manageable and solvable chunks

Learn/communicate the games rules

Generalisation

Apply and reuse existing strategies to solve a new (yet similar) challenge

Puzzle games may focus on reconstructing already decomposed objects

Since the launch of the new computing curriculum there has been an influx of new EduTech resources, and the games sector has not remained untouched by it all. Games such as: Daisy the Dino, A.L.E.X, Lightbot, Code Warriors, Code Kingdom, amongst others have flooded the market with games now available across platforms. Used appropriately they can add value to lessons and help reinforce the concepts that you are trying to teach. However, the EduTech games focus solely on developing programming skills; no one seems to have tackled the other aspects of the curriculum yet.

But this isn't just about the EduTech game market. Almost all games do in fact involve some element of strategic problem-solving, or more broadly computational thinking. They have value, and are worth considering as valuable curriculum resources. Games also can act as a nice crossover between subjects. For example, consider the games below:

- SimCity BuildIt – there are strong links here to geography, economics and citizenship with the game's emphasis on developing and governing your own city and making it successful both in trade and keeping your citizens happy. In fact the game has shown such strong correlation with education that a SimCity Edu version was built, with problem-solving challenges and resources developed for classrooms. One example of such a resource is the Pollution Challenge which connects Computational Thinking with Geography.[33]
- Pokemon Go – could easily be used as part of geography lessons with its built in GPS and mapping abilities. Using the Pokemon statistics can also tie in easily with mathematics.

The power of the video game is within its very nature. It provides a visual representation of a real or imagined environment, it's a safe place to try out new things, master new skills, and fail (several times) in the process. For some games, the player progresses in a very linear fashion. So for example, in games such as Candy Crush and Plants Vs Zombies there is a clear defined level. Each level has its own defined game screen, with a challenge (of increasing difficulty) that needs to be solved. Everyone

---

33. www.instituteofplay.org/work/projects/simcityedu-games or access via
www.glasslabgames.org/games/SC

plays the game in the same way, every player receives the same challenges and in the same order. Other games, are not defined in such a linear fashion. These are referred to as Sandbox games or Open Worlds. In these games the player defines what happens next through the choices they make. Overall challenges and problems are still set, and while these may start out the same over the duration of the game they may diverge according the player's behaviour. One of the earliest and perhaps most famous of these games is Grand Theft Auto, although one of the first recognised Sandbox game is considered to be Hunter (1991) which is a 3D action adventure game where a player navigates a series of islands.

Sandbox games like Minecraft provide a rich world for players to make their creations come to life. The link between a game such as Minecraft and computing has been well reported with teachers sharing examples of how they have used Minecraft to illustrate and deliver topics such as Logic Gates for GCSE Computing, or Vikings and Tudors for KS3 History. Players are able to create their own worlds, visit locations built by their friends or play in story mode which follows a narrative and fend off dangerous challenges. Teachers, also, are able to use Minecraft to set up worlds, challenges and problems which tackle and demonstrate key computing concepts for their students to explore and potentially providing fantastic links to other subjects enabling a cross-curricular play-based learning approach to take place.

In these games, no two players may experience the same journey through the game. Players create and define their own experiences and choose how to progress. These games may set loose challenges or objectives to complete within the game, but inherently it is up to the user how long they take to complete it, and often these games provide several modes of play.

Sandbox games all provide a rich world within which learners can explore their creativity. These environments can easily be used to explore a range of subject concepts. For example, people have used Minecraft to:

- Teach computing concepts such as data representation and machine architecture. There are numerous YouTube videos showing simulated variations of the Central Processing Unit.

- Demonstrate Mathematical concepts, such as volume and capacity, algebra
- Visualise Scientific concepts such as understanding DNA, the speed of light and many more
- Teach events in History such as World War Two
- Understand key texts in English Literature, such as an animated sequence of Hamlet
- Simulate a range of religious environments to give learners a greater awareness of religious beliefs and practices

In fact, Minecraft has been so successful in supporting education that Microsoft have released Minecraft Edu, and with it a whole library of lesson plans and resources for every subject.

Another great example is Big Bang Legends where the aim is for learning to become a by-product of having fun. Big Bang Legends is a casual but challenging slingshot puzzler game. The game teaches about the periodic table, particle physics and atomic compositions, and is suitable for children aged six and over. The characters are based on elements from the periodic table – giving new meaning to a 'physics-based game'. There are puzzles to solve, anti-matter monsters to destroy and rewards to be picked up. Players can collect and upgrade 118 unique characters with different powers. This introduces the elements on the periodic table and teaches the names of elements and their symbols.

Lightneer, developers of Big Bang Legends, have focused on effectively combining essential gameplay and learning elements. For example:

- Learning: using protons to build atoms
- Learning: element usage information (e.g. helium used in balloons, lithium in medication)
- Learning: history of the Universe (in sagamap)
- Learning and gameplay: element special abilities (e.g. gases can float over gaps)
- Learning and gameplay: nuclear fusion
- Learning and gameplay: using atom classes to pass levels (for

example, solving a problem requiring the use of a noble gas or an alkali metal)

Lightneer's reasoning for this approach is their simple claim that innumerable people in the world struggle with learning and understanding. Education is broken: according to recent research, 25% of school kids are bored to death and almost 50% of them have no understanding of why they go to school. Educational systems are not well-equipped to deal with the learning challenges set out by a world that changes faster every day. Lightneer's mission, therefore, is to make learning accessible and engaging to everybody in the world. Lightneer believes in learning games. They recognise that games are an amazing platform for learning, and every great game is a learning experience. Learning games need to be as much fun to play as the best games out there. They specifically design their learning games so that, in addition to teaching subjects such as physics, modern foreign languages, history etc., they stand on their own when compared to the best games of the world. In other words, people should want to play their games simply because they are just good games, regardless of the learning value.

The possibilities are as endless as the games. With the development of new games come new ideas, new challenges and new problems to solve. The ability for games to fuse together the STEM subjects with computing and art enable them to become the perfect place for learners to explore new ideas through play, merging together computational thinking and creativity.

Take for example the games listed opposite. Each one of these, while not considered to be an educational game, does in fact enable players to use and potentially develop some area of computational thinking. Each game in the list has been flagged for the computational thinking opportunities that it brings with it. It is important to note that these are by no means exhaustive or exclusive; it is perfectly possible for a teacher to use the game in a way that meets strands of computational thinking that are different to those mapped opposite.

		Computational Thinking Strands					
App	Developer	Logical Reasoning/ Problem-solving	Algorithmic Thinking	Abstraction	Generalisation	Decomposition	Evaluation
The Room	Fireproof Games	✓	✓			✓	
Plants Vs Zombies 2	PopCap	✓	✓	✓	✓		✓
Angry Birds	Rovio Entertainment Ltd.	✓	✓	✓	✓		
Fallout Shelter	Bethesda	✓					✓
Wuzzit Trouble	Brainquake Inc.	✓					✓
SimCity Buildit	EA Swiss Sarl	✓				✓	✓
Big Bang Legends	Lightneer	✓	✓		✓		
Hakitzu	Kuato Games	✓	✓		✓	✓	✓
The Foos	codeSpark	✓	✓			✓	✓
Tynker	Tynker	✓	✓	✓	✓	✓	✓
Game Press	UntitledD	✓	✓	✓	✓	✓	✓
Hopscotch	Hopscotch Tech	✓	✓	✓	✓	✓	✓
Robot School	Next is Great	✓	✓	✓	✓	✓	✓
Rollercoaster Tycoon	Chris Sawyer/ Atari	✓					✓
Hearthstone: Heroes of Warcraft	Blizzard Entertainment	✓	✓				
Minecraft	Mojang/ Microsoft Studios	✓			✓		✓
Unroll Me	Turbo Chilli Pty Ltd	✓	✓				

Does that mean we can simply let learners play the game and they'll develop the computational thinking for themselves? Chances are, probably not. This is where the teacher comes in. Players simply play the game, it's an immersive activity and few players will stop play to evaluate the skills that they are developing as a result. Therefore the teacher's role here as a facilitator is ideal. Through key questions at timely intervals they ensure learners focus on what they are learning and can provide the necessary trigger points to help them consolidate their understanding of the concepts covered. In short they provide the framework within which students can structure their learning.

Take for example the game Angry Birds. The most common format of the game requires players to select the angle at which to slingshot their bird to destroy a structure that is at some distance. The highest points in the game are awarded when the structure is destroyed in the fewest attempts. Mastery in the game requires the player to choose not only the correct angle at which to sling the bird but also to target the most effective point within the structure that will bring the whole thing crumbling down (there is little point in throwing your bird against a solid and stable brick wall!). Maths, Physics and Engineering teachers will no doubt begin to see the relevance to their subjects. There is potential here for the game to support the teaching of mathematics, especially through its use of angles. It also uses an understanding of physics and elements of engineering in ensuring your bird makes the most destructive impact. However, through gameplay alone the student will not become experts in those STEM subjects. They will not stop to assess or consider what mathematical knowledge they have applied to reach their new high score. By bringing the game into the classroom the teacher can build the game into the learning required enabling students to see the game in a new light. Through discussions they can examine how they managed to effectively complete particular levels, what algorithmic thinking they might have applied and whether or not they were generalising their solutions from one level to another.

Video games move away from the more didactic teaching pedagogy, and put the power of learning back in the hands of the children. They enable pupil-led learning to take place, which in turn facilitates the development of creativity and computational thinking skills.

Video games and cross-curricular creative computing

Games > Literacy + Computing + Art

A good game will have a good story behind it and if a story is good enough and delivered well then it can engage anyone. An engaging story can be just what a teacher needs to excite learners and motivate them with their creative writing. Games such as Tomb Raider have had such compelling stories behind them that they have engaged mass audiences through spin-offs which include Hollywood blockbuster movies, a comic book series and four official novels.

Tomb Raider immerses the player into the game world, which in turn requires them to play with the eyes and ears of the game character. This immersion into a creative world can provide just the hook learners need to inspire them in a variety of ways.

One significant potential impact is that games provide the leverage and materials to enable learners to develop their own creative writing skills. All the most popular titles employ video games writers who will develop scripts and write narratives for video games. They aren't too far removed from film scripts, and are simply another form of creative writing or written prose. Likewise, given the right set of resources English teachers could easily use video games as their focus or in support of studying a topic in English Literature. For example, English Literature students are often required to study Wilfred Owen, who is a famous poet from the First World War. The First World War is also studied as part of History lessons in secondary schools. There are many games such as Valiant Hearts (a video game published by Ubisoft where the player takes on a character during WWI) that could support both subjects.

James Gee has developed a body of work arguing that video games help to develop a learner's literacy and cognitive thinking skills. He argues that the theory of learning in good video games is as close as you can get to the best theories of learning in cognitive science. That may seem as a surprise, but the truth is AAA games are often long and challenging to play. An average game can take anywhere from 30–100 hours to complete; and yet players will continue to play them. Often and sometimes with a dedication that they may rarely show in the classroom! Why? Well a game simply won't sell if it isn't challenging enough, the players demand it. How many students demand more difficult and challenging lessons? A game must have learning principles built into its design, for example a game's initial levels are based around teaching the player how to play the game and develop new skills that will help them in later levels. You need to master the initial levels if you are going to succeed at later ones.

How does school compare with that? School is based around learning theories and principles that were developed in a time very different from that experienced by students of today. Current students' lives are immersed in a modern high-tech world where information and learning comes from an increasing number of sources. Yet rather than capitalise on making the best of this new technology, all too often schools shy away from it all, doing their students a disservice. Gee calls for a move away from the drill and test method of teaching, into a form that enables collaborative and active learning. He recommends that the learning features players will see and experience in good video games are all well supported by research in the learning sciences; all of which should be presented in schools.

LEGO have also made similar arguments in their research which looks at the constructionist and constructivist approaches to learning. The arguments put forward by them support the arguments presented in this book and by Gee. They believe in seven guiding principles which make teaching productive and learning effective.

The seven principles are:

1. Learning happens most effectively when learners are motivated to engage with the learning.

2. Learners should be given opportunities and resources for hands-on exploration and first-hand experiences with the learning content.

3. Learning becomes deeper when learners are facilitated to engage in reflection concerned with the explorations and experiences they have had.

4. Learners continue their learning trajectory when they feel they have mastered and own the learned knowledge and skills.

5. Learners learn more when they are involved in a playful approach to learning.

6.   Learning is enhanced through collaborative experiences.

7.   Learning and creativity are linked strongly to each other – especially when learning is looked at from a future perspective.

These principles are presented as the 4Cs; a dynamic process meant to scaffold and enable all seven aspects of effective learning experiences.

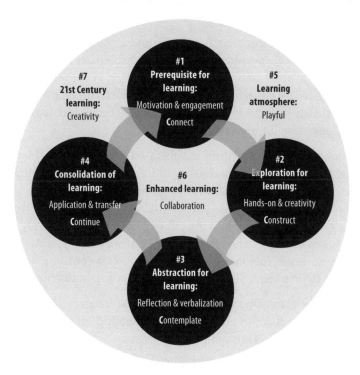

Figure 7: Making Teaching Productive and Learning Effective – LEGO's 4Cs[34]

LEGO may have been talking about playing with bricks, but it's still playing and learning through play and hence can apply just as much to learning through the application of video games as it does to LEGO bricks. For example, let's consider the seven principles:

34. Reproduced from LEGO Education (2015): 'Why the LEGO Education approach to teaching and learning works!', education.lego.com/en-gb/about-us

1. Pre-requisite for Learning: Motivation and engagement – video games encourage an intrinsic motivation amongst the players to develop their skills, perform better and complete the game.

2. Exploration for learning: Hands on and Creativity – video games are definitely creative, and used in the right ways can inspire a lot of creativity too. The hands-on element simply goes without saying!

3. Abstraction for learning: Reflection and verbalisation – a player may reflect on their performance and progress either independently or with their peers in order to perform better. However, this is where a teacher is invaluable as they can support and enable structured and timely reflection to help the concepts being learned develop to a deeper level of understanding.

4. Consolidation of learning: Application and transfer – players will use the skills they have developed in one game and become better over time, not just within that game but across games too. The eSports industry is full of players that have become so good at it that they are able to make a living out of it! The same can apply across a range of examples though. If using games as an inspirational hook for a series of lessons then the learning can continue beyond the game to help the students apply what they learnt during game play.

5. Learning atmosphere: Playful – self-explanatory, but yes, video games are a form of play, and therefore build on children's natural abilities to learn through play.

6. Enhanced Learning: Collaboration – learning with others is a natural way to learn, and 21st Century skills are going to require co-creation and collaboration. Many games require effective team work; consider some of the most major sports such as football, cricket and rugby, all of which require collaboration and team work if participants are to win the game.

7. 21st Century Learning: Creativity – games inspire creativity, and help players/students make their own creative leaps to help themselves discover new concepts and ideas. Learners need to be able to think for themselves.

Game-based learning can transform education

Using games to transform education is something that many people across the world have made a start on already. From the Redbridge Games Network made up entirely of teachers, to the Institute of Play in New York or the Playful Learning Centre in Helsinki; all have made great strides in proving that games truly can transform not just the classroom but the entire school environment. Games and the power of play can help transform students into lifelong learners with a natural love for learning.

The Redbridge Games Network

The Redbridge Games Network is set up and run by a collection of schools in the London Borough of Redbridge. The thought leaders behind the project are teachers who are essentially interested in games and the possibilities they bring to learning. They continue to run several projects and share their outcomes and thoughts at redbridgegamesnetwork. blogspot.co.uk.

Their site is a repository of ideas that are the result of practitioner research in the classroom – they are tried and tested, they work. Being mainly primary practitioners the teachers investigated the use of popular entertainment games to increase learning and engagement with a range of subjects. Here are some of the ideas that they developed:

Game/Platform	Suggestions for Classroom Use	Subject
Nintendo Wii Golf	Practise subtraction by working out the length of the shot	Maths
Nintendo Wii Super Paper Mario	Explain 2D & 3D with Super Paper Mario – the game allows you to flip perspectives	Maths
Nintendo Wii Bowling	Practise number bonds. Children can write down number sentences and three part sums to calculate scores	Maths
Nintendo Wii Bowling	Data collection exercise to help calculate averages and range	Maths
Nintendo Wii Mario Kart	Use different tracks to explore different worlds and experiment with descriptive language. Creating new Mario characters and practise writing their descriptions	Literacy
Nintendo DS/DSi	Use the Picto Chat facility for collaborative writing	Literacy

Professor Layton & the Curious Village	Solve puzzles, create puzzles, write character descriptions and make up new characters, draw a map of the village	Cross-curricular including: English, Geography, Maths
Nintendo DS/DSi Brain Training	Ideal for mental maths practice – create a classroom league	Maths
Nintendo Wii – Wild Earth African Safari	Learning about animal adaptation and interdependence and habitats	Science
Nintendo Wii – Wild Earth African Safari	Creating non chronological reports, diary entries, fact files, descriptive narrative and note taking	Literacy
Nintendo Wii Fit	Class Yoga	PE
Nintendo Wii Sports Resort	Describing the settings and features of an island	Literacy, Geography

The ideas presented here are just a brief condensed list of a full collection of resources presented on the group's sites and blogs. Their experiences and mapping clearly demonstrate that in these cases games are able to enrich learning experiences for the pupils, and, in many cases, they are helping to raise the achievement of lower ability pupils.

Amazing things can truly happen when you are hooked into what you are learning.

Institute of Play

The Institute of Play is based in New York and receives support and funding from a number of partners including EA Games, the Bill & Melinda Gates Foundation, Intel and many such others. Their work is truly transformational and is guided by the following values:

- **Value People** – people have inborn creativity and dignity with the power to design, build and rebuild ingenious systems that enrich and give life meaning.

- **Value Play** – where people find permission to take risks, to fail and have fun trying again and again. In play people are empowered to move freely through rigid structures, like rules, cultural norms or personal belief systems. In that freedom is the potential for transformation, for a break-through beyond whatever confines us.

- **Value possibility** – which exists in the moment of break-through, when a game's structure and rules suddenly shift. To experience possibility is to be inspired to engage fully, to co-create the world we share to play in.
- **Value partnership** – and seize opportunities to play with others to enlarge our work and enrich our process.

The values held by the Institute in many ways sum up many of the key messages of this book. That people ARE creative; that play enables us to take risks, fail and have fun while doing so; and that all this helps improve and transform our educational experiences to help us become better lifelong learners.

Researchers the world over are arguing that 21st Century skills require higher order thinking, creative problem-solving amongst others. The Institute of Play proposes that games naturally support this; that they are designed by their very nature to create compelling worlds and problems, and that players understand and resolve these through their own self-directed exploration of the virtual space. Game mechanics provide necessary scaffolding to help players understand how to operate within the space and where to go next. They create a compelling environment which drives players on to continue to master skills in order to master the game itself. These are all attributes that should be synonymous with learning and education. It is why many experts argue that games are inherently learning systems.

Games involve play, and are in fact social activities. Players learn as much from each other as they do in their own explorations. It is one environment where they will willingly share and exchange knowledge, skills and ideas. If we can duplicate this in everyday classrooms, then we can break down barriers and accelerate learning.

To help implement their values and beliefs the Institute of Play designs games and classroom resources in a variety of formats. Some of these include:

- The online adventure game Gamestar Mechanic. Players learn computational thinking and design by designing, repairing and playing games.

- Glasslab, which is a research and development effort which explores the potential for existing and commercially successful digital games to serve as potent learning environments. One of the outcomes of this research has been the creation of SimCityEDU, which links the popular Sim game to different educational curricula.

- Quest Schools is a model for schools to operate in a completely re-imagined way that extends the learning beyond the walls of the school to engage students in a way that is exciting, empowering and culturally relevant. The model sets a unique challenge to students on a termly basis and brings the subjects together in order to resolve it in a cross-curricular way.

- Teacher Quest works with Quest Schools to help teachers design activities using the pedagogical power of games to increase student motivation and engagement.

- Print & Play Games are a series of games that teachers can download, print and play within the classroom. They may be board games or card games, but each one focuses on a different topic. Initial games available for download are Absolute Blast, which teaches maths, and Socratic Smackdown, which is a discussion based humanities game.

Playful Learning Centre

The Playful Learning Centre is based in Helsinki and carries out research and development on using the power of play to transform learning and educational practice. Their core goals can be summarised as:

- offering new conceptualisations of play and playfulness within the context of 21st Century lifelong and lifewide learning

- developing research-based understandings of playful learning activities in formal, non-formal and informal contexts of learning

- developing new pedagogic knowledge and practices to support the professional development of teachers and education professionals in fostering playful learning in their communities and institutions

- uncovering conditions for transformative co-creation processes of playful learning solutions in multidisciplinary teams
- supporting capacity building and the development of new industrial-education relationships for the co-creation of playful learning solutions
- boosting and opening new educational markets for playful learning solutions

In collaboration with Rovio (the makers of Angry Birds) the centre has developed an innovative learning environment, a 'playground' which they use as a living lab for playful learnings solutions research, development and education. The programme works as an accelerator between academic research and educational games focusing on combining the innovation of games companies such as Rovio with its already high level of educational expertise to help shape Finland into a leading country for playful learning solutions. Therefore, the centre brings together kindergartens, schools, museums, libraries, science centres, universities, start-up companies and more to develop their ideas in playful learning. It's an interdisciplinary and a co-creative approach to making and testing solutions. So far their work has included:

- digital games design and testing
- playful learning, pedagogy and teacher education
- creativity
- developing new knowledge and innovations on playful learning

Phenomenal Education

While researching computing education I have encountered the abbreviation PBL several times. What does PBL stand for? That's a good question, up until now I've seen the following meanings:

- problem-based learning
- play-based learning
- project-based learning
- And now … phenomenon-based learning

While there are key differences between the various approaches, there is one striking feature that runs through all four. All four approaches emphasise student-led learning and the teacher's role as a facilitator supporting an interdisciplinary approach.

We've already previously discussed problem-based and play-based learning, so now let's turn our attention to phenomenon-based learning.

Phenomenon-based learning is being developed in Finland and is being rolled out nationally across all schools in the country. Each school is required to deliver at least one module of phenomenon-based learning a year and its goal is to develop deep learning and understanding amongst their students.

The main structure is quite simple. Students work alongside their teachers to pose key questions that concern them, something that they have a genuine interest in. The class uses an interdisciplinary approach to analyse a real life scenario or phenomenon. This single topic will be considered using several different approaches to help students arrive at the answers that they are looking for. Students themselves are responsible for first identifying and then filling the gaps in their own knowledge. Researchers and developers of the approach believe that this then helps build in the authentic learning of genuine work practices. They are learning what they need to learn in a way that is relevant and makes sense to them, not for example learning a topic out of context just for the sake of it or because that is when it happened to be written into the scheme of work.

These 'newer' approaches to learning are all exciting, somewhat experimental but also have a great potential to transform educational practices. Coupled with play-based learning they can bring the magic back into the classroom, engaging disengaged students and developing a love of lifelong learning.

Combining game-based learning along with one of the PBL approaches can create some interesting classroom ideas. One interesting example of gamification of lessons is Classcraft.[35] Classcraft takes inspiration from well known games such as World of Warcraft and applies the mechanics to a classroom situation. A teacher sets up a class, and divides them into

---

35. classcraft.com

teams. Each student chooses a character for themselves from one of three categories; Healer, Mage or Warrior. The students then gain rewards for things such as submitting their homework on time and answering questions correctly, or face a consequence for arriving late to the lesson. The teacher customises the rewards and consequences that enable students to unlock new powers to progress in the game.

> *"That's what makes Classcraft different and innovative.*
> *Rather than being a simple system for scoring points,*
> *Classcraft empowers students to take control of their*
> *learning process. It fosters significant relationships by*
> *reinforcing teamwork and collaboration rather than competition.*
> *It's pervasive and affects all aspects of a student's life. It's fun*
> *because unexpected things happen during gameplay."*[36]

Another resource is Education City.[37] Education City has a range of interactive activities and games for use in primary schools and at home with families. Learners work along a progression route at their own pace, with activities divided into subject specific modules. Teachers can track student progress.

While Classcraft turns the entire experience into a single exclusive game for which all the students in the class are players that can strategise with each other and against competing teams, Education City takes a different approach by building in games and games based activities for students to interact with to help illustrate and demonstrate a range of concepts.

We all know that while one resource may work brilliantly for one class, it may not necessarily do the job for another. The important point is to find out what motivates and engages our students as well as what their educational needs are. Engaging, motivating and inspiring our students is critical if we are going to embed lifelong learning skills within them. Combining computational thinking with creativity and play-based learning can help us 'think outside the box' when it comes to devising effective lesson plans.

---

36. classcraft.com/gamification
37. www.educationcity.com

Creative qualities are like muscles that need to be trained and built over the course of time. The more opportunities we give our learners to flex these muscles and utilise them to expand the possibilities and understanding of concepts, ideas and the world around them, the stronger, more creative, effective and efficient they will become. It is when these qualities become embedded that our learners' true creative capacity will shine through.[38]

A multitude of lecture talks, conferences, CPD events and other media deal with issues surrounding the need to increase the take up of STEM subjects by students, and to increase the number of girls taking STEM subjects. Suffice to say, that while many of these mediums discuss policies and clever strategies some of which do work and others of which do not, the answer, I believe, lies in the lesson itself. Many students, once given a choice of subjects, will not choose subjects that they don't enjoy. If students enjoy the subject, then they will choose to continue with it. It's really as simple as that.

---

38. www.lifehack.org/articles/lifestyle/your-creative-genius-mindset-the-essential-qualities-for-outside-the-box-thinking.html

Chapter 6

Interactive Fiction in Education

Learning is a two-way process between the student and the educator, and the best, most rewarding teaching and learning experiences today are interactive, as any Ofsted inspector will tell you. Children are not expected to remain passive in lessons; they are supposed to be actively engaged with the topic being covered, whether that be conducting an experiment into static electricity in a Science lesson, or discussing Henry VIII's reasons for breaking the Church of England from Rome in a History lesson.

It is not so much that interaction is a new tool to be used in the classroom, it is more that we have only recently rediscovered something which was the norm for so many centuries, and yet which became lost in the mists of time. And it is thanks to a number of notable pioneers that it was rediscovered at all.

Interactive fiction is one powerful way to provide interaction that is both playful and encourages creativity and literacy. It's also a great way to develop computational thinking skills.

The birth of the gamebook

The publication in 1982 of *The Warlock of Firetop Mountain*, written by Steve Jackson and Ian Livingstone (also co-author of this book), and the advent of the *Fighting Fantasy* series, started a playground revolution. *Fighting Fantasy* sparked a generation of readers who immersed themselves in interactive worlds of monsters and magic. The series has sold more than 18 million copies worldwide to date in over 30 languages.

Fighting Fantasy is a series of gamebooks in which YOU, the reader, are the Hero. What is so compelling about *Fighting Fantasy* is that the reader affects the outcome of the story by assuming the role of the hero, and choosing which paths to follow by navigating numbered paragraphs. A game system is attached to the branching narrative to allow combat with monsters and character development. *Fighting Fantasy* is in effect the gamification of literature – interactive fiction and game rules delivered via analogue hypertext.

Because of the branching narrative, there are many ways to navigate a *Fighting Fantasy* gamebook, but usually only one successful way. Some choices lead to the readers 'dying' at the hands of some gruesome beast. But nearly all readers cannot wait to start again, compelled by the challenge and the puzzle-solving aspects of the books. Through the different choices made, readers' experiences are unique to them. The narrative is related in the second person present tense, and readers often talk about their adventures in the 'I' form as though they were there.

Giving control of the story to the readers by allowing them to direct the narrative and make the decisions is empowering. Interactive worlds come alive in readers' minds and have a powerful effect on children's imaginations. Readers feel like they are actually taking part in heroic adventures in post-apocalyptic worlds or fighting gruesome monsters in dangerous fantasy lands.

Never before had such an interactive story been published, in book form at least, with a set of self-contained game rules attached. Having created the gamebook genre, *Fighting Fantasy* went on to popularise the genre in the UK, the Commonwealth, and the world. The idea has been aped and mimicked many times since, but *Fighting Fantasy* books remain, in most people's minds, the best. And despite first being published in the 1980s, these gamebooks have not dated at all, since they were set in either fantastical worlds, or far-fetched futuristic ones, in the first place.

With their heady mix of exciting, action-packed adventure, and decision-making that put the fate of the world in younger readers' hands, the books were a worldwide hit.

One of the aspects of *Fighting Fantasy* gamebooks that made them so popular and so memorable was the artwork, which was seen as being mature, monstrous and sometimes just downright gruesome. This was something people weren't used to seeing in children's books at the time. It caused consternation among some and sparked controversy in others, who vehemently shared their outspoken views in the press and even during radio phone-ins. There was even a petition wanting them banned. But this backlash only came from adults, who feared what they did not understand. Children loved the books, and the fact that in some cases their parents didn't like them only added to the underground appeal of books with such sensational titles as *The Warlock of Firetop Mountain, Forest of Doom, City of Thieves, Deathtrap Dungeon, The Citadel of Chaos, House of Hell, Temple of Terror* and *The Creature of Havoc*.

Despite the criticism of *Fighting Fantasy* when the books were first published in the 1980s, a 2014 study suggested that interactive fiction increases language and literacy skills. It concluded that children, especially those with learning difficulties, benefit more from an interactive reading experience than from a passive one.

Interactive fiction in the here and now

Back in the 1980s, when they first came out, *Fighting Fantasy* gamebooks were feared and criticised by some parents and teachers, just as with so many new things. But *Fighting Fantasy* also came to the attention of teachers nationwide because of the peculiar effect it was having on their pupils – particularly the male ones. It was inspiring boys to read, and not only that, but creating an enthusiasm for reading. A level of energy and passion that had formerly been reserved for talking about what they watched on TV the night before, or the latest unmissable football match, was now being expended talking about the characters and monsters from a series of fantasy books.

Fighting Fantasy gamebooks made reading an enjoyable interactive experience, and for children who were not necessarily natural readers – both boys and girls – this was a massive boost. *Fighting Fantasy* put the reader squarely at the centre of the action, encouraging them to choose their own path forward through the book. This was a sure-fire method for getting readers engrossed in the story and to really care about what was happening.

But the generation of children who discovered *Fighting Fantasy* back in the 1980s have grown up in the intervening 35 years to become the teachers and parents of a new generation of children, and, quite rightly, gamebooks have finally been welcomed into educational establishments with open arms.

What makes interactive fiction such a wonderful educational resource and learning tool is the way in which it engages a reader like nothing else, particularly when so many children today learn how to play video games before they learn to read.

First of all, there are the plots. Exciting, dramatic, heroic, epic in scope and personal in their execution. Then there is the fact that the reader is the hero, placing them at the heart of the story. As a direct consequence of this, the reader is instrumental in deciding what happens next and so shapes the course of the story directly.

Fighting Fantasy adventures are illustrated throughout with suitably hideous monsters and nefarious villains, and these help to make a bizarre fantasy world the reader's reality for the duration of the reading experience.

Another benefit of gamebooks is the very structure of the books themselves. The individual references, or paragraphs, which are in the main relatively short, ensure that the reader isn't put off by having to wade through chapters ten pages, or more, long. Also, having to continually turn backwards and forwards to different pages throughout the book, the reader never really has a clear idea of how far through the story they are, and so aren't put off by the feeling that they have been reading all day and are only a quarter of the way through the narrative.

Last of all, but by no means least, there is the fact that the reader is playing a game as well as reading a book. *Fighting Fantasy* gamebooks allow the reader to enjoy the tactical sensation of rolling dice, their pulse racing as they await the outcome.

It is now well documented how successfully gamebooks enthuse children, making them actively interested in reading, sustaining that interest, and thereby helping to improve their literacy levels. Not only that, *Fighting Fantasy* books helps to inspire creative writing and artistic endeavour.

SKILL, STAMINA and LUCK

The benefits gained from reading interactive fiction are now recognised by educationalists, and they are manifold. Children who participate in an interactive story-telling experience develop better decision-making skills, improved problem-solving skills, and enhanced sequencing skills. The process encourages creative thinking and has children understanding the principles of logic, whilst also empowering them as decision-makers and narrative-creators themselves. It gives more meaning to the exercises they undertake and keeps them engaged, all of this taking place within a framework of active learning.

Many people underestimate the importance of learning decision-making skills, and they do so at their peril. To prove the point, *Fighting Fantasy* gamebooks have been used in young offender institutions, specifically to teach the young people temporarily resident there – who are not naturally good decision-makers – the importance of reasoned decision-making and understanding, as well as predicting, what the resulting consequences may be.

In case anyone still needed persuading that interactive fiction should be used in a teaching environment, its very interactivity engages children, putting them at the core of a child-centred, game-based curriculum.

Studies carried out by cognitive theorists have also shown that people who play interactive fiction games, as opposed to readers of linear fiction, spontaneously create spatial mental representations of the world in which the story is taking place. The reason for this is to help the player navigate throughout that world, with the player internalising a great portion of the spatial world they experience in the game.

And yet even in this digital age, there is still a place for the analogue reading experience, just as there is still a place for books in the classroom. Indeed, the very tactile experience of reading a book, especially flicking from paragraph to paragraph, is very different from that of reading a story on a screen. When presented with information as part of an app, for example, the reader tends to jump to the list of choices at the bottom, often tapping on one without reading the preceding text which may give clues as to which option would be the most sensible choice. However, when presented with the printed page, the reader will more often than not read through the text from top to bottom, only deciding where to go next having taken note of any hints present in the passage above.

A walk in The Forest of Doom

There are all manner of activities you can undertake with children, with interactive fiction as the focus or as a jumping-off point, from reading through a gamebook with a group, where the students take turns to make the choices they encounter as the adventure proceeds, to designing an alternative cover for a favourite adventure, to the children writing their own adventures and drawing the monsters.

Although you can of course use interactive fiction story-telling techniques with children of any age, as long as they are old enough to enjoy ordinary story books, the *Fighting Fantasy* series is most popular among children aged between 8 and 12; in other words, children who are already literate.

Take, for example, Ian Livingstone's *The Forest of Doom*. Despite having the word 'Doom' in the title, the setting of a forest, at first glance, appears relatively benign, and it may be for this reason that the book has proved as popular with girls as it has with boys since it first came out back in 1983. It has remained one of the most popular titles in the *Fighting Fantasy* series and now even exists in app form (courtesy of indie digital developer Tin Man Games).

In *The Forest of Doom*, the adventurer has to brave the perils of Darkwood Forest in order to recover the pieces of the stolen Hammer of Stonebridge, an ancient artefact fashioned by the Dwarfs to protect their village from the predations of Hill Trolls. Before setting out on their mission, the hero visits the wise old wizard Yaztromo to glean vital information about the forest and its inhabitants, and to equip themselves for the adventure that lies ahead.

There is a plethora of literacy lessons that can be spun out of the adventure that is contained within the pages of the book. Before you even start reading through the adventure with your class you could ask them to write down their predictions as to what the adventure might be about, based on its name alone.

During the course of reading the book you could get them to write biographies and backstories for the people the hero meets along the way – for example, the arm-wrestling barbarian Quin, describing how he came to be in the forest and in possession of a phial of Dust of Levitation – or you could stop half way through a scene, and ask them to write the ending.

Once you have completed the adventure, you might ask the children to write a set of instructions directing someone safely through the forest, from one side to the other, and warning them about the dangers they may face along the way, or they could write a letter to Yaztromo, telling the old wizard about how they fared in the forest, recounting the story that they experienced whilst playing through the adventure.

In fact the books support not just literacy but also the wider school remit of developing a well-rounded individual who is able make reasoned ethical and moral judgements. The books present a range of problems that students explore the answer to. The problems often replicate moral and ethical dilemmas that students make, choices which in real life can be quite difficult to make. However, the game- and story-based environment allows students to effectively remove themselves emotionally from the story and explore a range of consequences from different actions taken in a safe environment.

However, one of the most rewarding, but also probably the most challenging, of exercises is to write a sample encounter, in which the children come up with the alternate options and outcomes to turn to themselves. And here's one way how to do it using *The Forest of Doom*. Of course any gamebook could be used in the same way.

The Forest of Doom Literacy Lesson Plan

The following is a plan for an hour-long literacy lesson that can be adapted to suit any Key Stage 2 class, or even a Key Stage 3 class.

Resources needed for the lesson:

The *Fighting Fantasy* gamebook *The Forest of Doom* by Ian Livingstone, paper, pencils, colouring pencils or pens, whiteboard or flipchart.

Key vocabulary:

Adjective, gamebook, branching, narrative, senses.

Teacher expectations:

By the end of the lesson the children will know what interactive fiction is, they will understand how to use adjectives to good effect, and they will be able to structure a simple branching narrative.

Success criteria:

The children must be able to choose words to suit the purpose of their writing, they should be able to structure a branching narrative, and may be able to write dramatic scenes within that narrative using appropriate vocabulary to describe what the hero of the adventure senses.

Introduction (5 minutes)

Ask the children if they know what an adventure gamebook is, or whether they have read any stories where the reader gets to choose what happens next.

For the benefit of those children who haven't, explain that in a gamebook (or other work of interactive fiction) the reader is the hero, choosing what happens in the story from a series of branching storylines. (This is what we mean by a branching narrative.)

First Activity (10 minutes)

Read an extract from *The Forest of Doom*, such as the encounter with the talking crow (starting at paragraph 160) or the meeting with Quin the strongman (which starts at paragraph 99). If you want to, you can roll dice to simulate the battles that take place in the book, and to make tests to see how lucky the hero is, but for convenience sake in a classroom situation (unless you're doing it as part of a numeracy lesson) take it that every test is passed and every battle is won automatically.

Each time you come to a choice, either ask an individual child what you should do, or take a vote of the whole class. Having played through a few different sections, the children will begin to see how the branching narrative works. You could even retrace your steps, keeping a finger in a previous page, to see what would have happened if they had made a different choice.

Second Activity (20 minutes)

Tell the children that they are going to write their own scene to fit into *The Forest of Doom*. One of the things that makes the popularity of *Fighting Fantasy* gamebooks so enduring are the monsters that the hero meets and has to battle, so tell the children that they need to create a monster for their scene too.

Get them to think about the sort of thing that might live in a forest, although it could live in a lake or river (or even in a network of caves or a dungeon under the forest), give their creature a name and come up with five adjectives to describe it. Having described it, they can then draw a picture of their monster.

If you like, and if you wanted to spend longer on this activity (spreading the whole exercise over several lessons rather than just one), you could create a *pro forma* for your students to fill in, with boxes for the monster's name, its description, habitat, favourite food, and useful advice for any adventurer unfortunate enough to encounter one whilst travelling through the forest.

Third Activity (30 minutes)

Divide the class into groups and get them to share their monstrous creations with each other. Then have them choose one, or possibly more, that they want to feature in their scene.

Model how to create a branching narrative on the whiteboard, or flipchart, by drawing a simple flowchart, explaining that every time there is a choice they need to create two (or more) alternative passages which will then lead to further choices.

As an example (and one you might want to use in your lesson) this is how the encounter with a Sting Worm breaks down in Ian Livingstone's *The*

Forest of Doom. (The numbers included in the flowchart below are the relevant numbered sections in the book.)

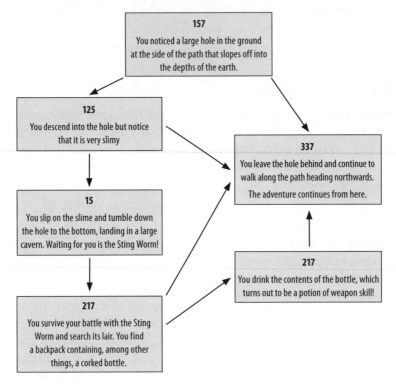

Figure 8: Flowchart for Ian Livingstone's Forest of Doom

This is a good example as it shows how with only six sections a simple branching narrative can be created but one which still offers the reader plenty of choice.

Having seen how a branching narrative is created, get the children, in their groups, to design their own brief scene, between six and ten sections long. Each child in the group can write one or two scenes each, but before doing so, they need to create a flowchart between them to show where the outcomes of their different decisions will take them.

You could obviously spend much more time on writing the individual sections of the story, considering how Ian Livingstone uses both descriptive language to help set the scene, and dramatic language to make the encounter with the Sting Worm exciting, and a little scary!

However, for a single lesson you could simply focus on the children constructing the narrative and point out that they could always re-write their passages, and embellish them, later on – adding more interesting adjectives and describing what the hero is seeing, feeling, hearing, smelling, and possibly even tasting.

The flowchart also clearly demonstrates the link to computing with this activity. This is an ideal opportunity to connect English and Computing lessons together. In their computing lessons, students can spend greater time focusing on the flowchart, and following different pathways through the story. There is potentially a lot of computational thinking that can be developed around this activity, if it was delivered with that in mind.

Plenary (5 minutes)

Ask the class for their feedback. Discuss how easy, or how hard, they found it to create a branching narrative. Ask them what they might do differently next time.

Assessment opportunities:

This activity lends itself particularly well to peer assessment. During the exercise the teacher can assess the children's progress as he or she circulates around the classroom, seeing how well they work together, considering their use of vocabulary, and their individual writing skills. The plenary session also provides an opportunity for assessing the children's speaking and listening skills.

Follow-up session

As mentioned above, this activity lends itself particularly well to peer assessment. The best way to accommodate this is in a follow-up session, either later on in the same day, or at another time in the week, maybe when the children have been able to finish their individual sections for homework.

Invite the children to share their scenes with the rest of class. Have each group come to the front of the class with individuals reading out their sections and then getting the rest of the class to choose which path to follow, from the range of choices presented to them.

Once each group has had a turn, ask the children what they liked about each other's work. Which ideas were particularly imaginative? Which scenes were particularly exciting? Which were their favourite monsters? Which encounters turned out differently from how they were expecting?

The children might also make suggestions as to how to develop scenes differently, or where to take the story next. From here, given enough time, the children could go on to write more scenes or, with a little help from their teacher, combine the scenes of the whole class to create one, much longer, branching narrative.

Going beyond the book

Although we have so far focused on the benefits to literacy of using interactive fiction – such as improving vocabulary and teaching story structure – gamebooks stimulate the reader's imagination in multiple ways, and so there are numerous other curriculum links that can be made, using the interactive fiction experience as a launching off point. Here are just some of them.

Art and Design: create new monsters for the adventurer to encounter; design a new cover for an existing gamebook.

Computing: use flowcharts and logic to consider structure. Producing a flowchart of the story can also help demonstrate graphing theory for older computing students.

Design and Technology: design and make dice, and dice rollers, or miniatures and scenery, or Adventure Sheets for record-keeping whilst playing the game; practise technical drawing skills.

Drama: re-play a favourite encounter from the gamebook, but acting it out as if it were a scene from a movie.

Geography: compass points; making and interpreting maps of places visited during the adventure, and using a key.

History: research the history of role-playing games such as *Dungeons & Dragons* and interactive fiction; find out more about the decade that spawned *Fighting Fantasy* gamebooks; research myths and legends to learn the origins of many favourite monsters. Or one exciting idea is to write a story about one real historical event and use the interactive story to show other possible futures.

Languages: look at the titles of foreign editions of *Fighting Fantasy* gamebooks and try to work out which ones they are, or see which have been changed and which are still the same, just written in another language.

Mathematics: straightforward addition and subtraction; calculating percentages and probabilities of random dice rolls; work on spatial awareness; measuring distances travelled in the game; calculating the area of dungeon chambers.

Music: listen to medieval music or soundtracks from fantasy films, and then create music to suit the fantasy setting of the gamebook; write a song in the style of a bard singing about the mighty deeds of a brave hero.

Physical Education: take part in a dungeon-style labyrinth obstacle course; practise fencing and archery skills.

Science: create a natural indicator 'magic potion' (using red cabbage) to detect acids and alkalis; grow crystals to use as set dressing in a game; research a subject of interest linked to the topic of the book, such as food webs in a forest habitat, in the case of *The Forest of Doom*.

Social Education: write a story about a real life situation and how the actions of one person can affect the feelings (and actions) of others.

Your adventure is only just beginning

Fighting Fantasy gamebooks – and other forms of interactive fiction, although *Fighting Fantasy* exemplifies it best – are both an unusual and interesting method of storytelling, and they are very useful when you wish to learn, or teach, how to construct plots.

In each book there are many ways to get through to the end. When someone sits down to write a story with a linear narrative, they are asking themselves the same questions you are posed as a reader of the *Fighting Fantasy* books. Do you take the path to the right? Do you use a sword or an axe? Do you kill the monster or try to talk to it? They are also interesting in that they demonstrate quite clearly that there can be many different endings to the same story.

So embrace the benefits of teaching and learning through interactive fiction. After all, the possibilities are quite literally endless!

Chapter 7

Putting it into Action

"Content and theory with the absence of the magic of teaching and learning means nothing … if we could transform teacher education to focus on teaching teachers how to create that magic then poof! We could make dead classes come alive, we could reignite imaginations, and we can change education." Christopher Emdin (2014)[39]

The following chapter aims to help teachers put into practice the theory of what has been covered in the book so far by providing practical activities that can be implemented in any classroom. The set of unplugged computing activities described all help to deliver and enhance computational thinking and 21st Century problem-solving skills. They enable the children to make their own discoveries and to learn through these using the power of play and creative computing. The teacher simply facilitates and guides their learning through this process. Extension activities and a discussion of the computational thinking involved is provided for each activity along with the key National Curriculum references. The practical activities are suitable for any age group, and can be easily adapted to fit in at the appropriate level. Extension tasks for each activity show how the work can be

---

39. Emdin, C. 2014. Teaching Teachers how to Create Magic. Ted talk:
    www.ted.com/talks/christopher_emdin_teach_teachers_how_to_create_magic

extended to help learners apply what they have learnt onto a digital implementation of their work.

However, these activities are by no means exhaustive, neither are they designed to be prescriptive in any way. Rather they are designed to provide teachers with a starting point, an activity to consider, test and try out with a range of different students. Experimentation and further innovation is highly encouraged!

The Computational Thinking Duck

Age group
Suitable for all ages

Resources required
- 6 LEGO Bricks per student (for the main activity)
- 2, 2x2 bricks (yellow)
- 1, 2x4 bricks (yellow)
- 1, 2x1 brick (yellow)
- 2, 2x3 flat plate bricks (yellow)
- A range of additional bricks for the extension activity
- A digital alternative to LEGO bricks is the Virtual LEGO Builder (www.buildwithchrome.com)

What to do
This activity uses LEGO bricks to help develop computational thinking and creativity skills through play. The students should be encouraged to tinker, play and explore ideas to discover key concepts for themselves. The role of the teacher in this activity is to facilitate that learning and help students realise their discoveries and to embed and solidify the knowledge that they have gained.

Create packs of the six bricks ensuring that each student has the two red and four yellow bricks to enable them to create their own duck. Ask students to build a duck, giving them no further instructions. Encourage them to get creative, see what they develop; each student should independently create their own duck and not attempt to follow their peers.

After each student has created their duck ask them to compare their ducks with those of their peers. This is a good point for discussion as all the ducks may well be different. Ask the students to examine their ducks, why is each one different? The answer is because of the instruction given. Simply saying "Make a duck" leaves how a duck should look open to interpretation. As humans we add our own prior knowledge and make the duck according to how we think it should look. However, computers do not have that ability, they simply follow the algorithm programmed within them.

The next part of the activity encourages students to examine algorithms in different forms.

Pair up students together. There are two distinct roles for the students to play, and both will take it in turns to play each role. One student will play the role of the 'programmer' and the other will be the 'human computer'. It will be the job of the programmer to describe their duck to the computer.

Verbal instructions

Instruct the students to first give their partner verbal instructions to recreate their duck. It is worth noting that this activity can be repeated several times with different levels of questioning attached to each. For example:

- *Round 1* – free discussion between the pair, no restrictions
- *Round 2* – allow the (student) computer to give feedback on whether or not they understood the instruction, but not ask any questions
- *Round 3* – the (student) computer gives no feedback on the instruction, they simply execute the instruction given as best as they can

Engage students in discussion about the algorithms they gave their partners:

- How successful was their algorithm?
- Did they have to refine their algorithm at all?
- How easy was it to describe their duck to enable their partner to recreate it?
- As the students worked through the rounds did the process become easier or more difficult?
- Round 2 and 3 begin to illustrate the importance of computer feedback and systems with well-designed error messages. What type of response from the student computer was the most helpful? Why?

Written instructions

Ask the students to write down the algorithm that would enable their partner to create the exact duck model that they have made.

Pair up students and tell them to swap instructions. Each student should test the instructions of their partner: are they able to recreate the same duck? Engage students in discussion about what they have found, for example some starting points may be:

- Give an example of a very good instruction – what made this a good instruction?
- Give an example of an instruction that was difficult to follow – why was this difficult?
- How long did it take to follow the algorithm?
- Were the instructions accurate?

Graphical instructions

When LEGO issue building instructions for their kits, the algorithms are graphical rather than text based. Why? Ask the students to examine existing LEGO building instructions (www.secure.us.lego.com/en-gb/service/buildinginstructions).

- What is common about each set of building instructions?

- What are the differences between each instruction set?
- Why are they easy to follow?

Engage students in discussion about the importance of good algorithms. What have they learnt from the tasks they have carried out so far?

Ask the students to draw their own building instructions for their duck and then test them on a new partner. Engage the students in another short discussion to evaluate the result of this test. Help draw out the key elements of the activity and what makes the graphical representation of the algorithm so effective for the duck building exercise.

Evaluating algorithms

Engage the students in discussion to compare the different algorithms that they have developed for their duck.

- Are the algorithms better written out or drawn?
- What difference does it make?
- Why?
- Which algorithm was easier to produce?
- Which algorithm was easier to follow?

The evaluation of the different algorithms can take a more formal approach by working with students to devise a set of evaluation criteria that they can then test. These criteria could include:

- The speed of the algorithm
  - the length of time it took to create the duck by following each algorithm
- The accuracy of the algorithm
  - Was the end result accurate?
  - How many errors were made by following the algorithm?
- How easy was the algorithm to follow?

Extended activities

There are a range of activities that can be carried out using different coloured six bricks. The activity carried out can be easily extended, with students developing their own versions. Try the activities below:

Ask students to pick their own six bricks and then:

- Use it to create an object, e.g. a tree
- Develop an algorithm for the object
- Give the bricks (without the algorithm) to another person
- Do they create the object identical to yours?
- Now try it with the algorithm? Does it work?

Links to Computational Thinking

Where is the computational thinking in this activity?

This activity uses a range of computational thinking techniques. The key skill developed here is algorithmic thinking, with students formulating their own instructions that may be simply sequential or follow logical operations. Students work with their verbal instructions to create them in written form, which then may begin to see the introduction of programming concepts such as loops/iteration.

The construction of the duck enables them to touch upon abstraction and decomposition. For example, they need to be able to identify the different parts of the duck that can be represented through the six bricks. While this in itself is decomposition, abstraction enables them to realise that they will not create an exact replica of the duck. Key details about the features of a duck will need to be ignored if they are going to create their own model replica using only six LEGO bricks. Teachers can engage in discussion to help students see what details they automatically began to ignore about ducks.

Continuous evaluation enables students to constantly test and debug their algorithms. Key discussions around the effectiveness of different algorithms enable them to see if they are fit for purpose. Were there alternative solutions, what did their peers come up with? These are all valuable considerations and it is important if possible to enable students to try and arrive at their own evaluation criteria; this may be specific for each individual or a collective effort by the class to arrive at a common set of criteria that they deem suitable.

Tip: to ensure everyone contributes to the common set of evaluation criteria, ask each student to write their top 3 most important evaluation criteria on Post-it notes and then to stick them onto the board/wall etc. The teacher can then use these to identify the most common suggestions (and the most important ones) to help devise the class set.

Recommended reading: Extend this with 6 Bricks

Did you enjoy this activity? This work has been inspired by the work of the LEGO Foundation and the 6 Bricks project. Find out more about the project and download further activities and classroom resources from: www.legofoundation.com/en-us/programmes/communities/six-bricks

The 6 Bricks booklet sets out a number of activities to help students develop their problem-solving, memory, creativity and movement skills. Many of these activities also serve as excellent ideas to help develop computational thinking, and delivered appropriately with the correct emphasis they will work for students of varying ages and abilities. Some of these activities have been pulled out below.

Back to Back

- Students stand back-to-back in pairs with the same three bricks
- One student builds a model and then explains to their partner how to build the same model

- The partner builds without looking or asking questions
- The pairs compare models and discuss how it went
- The activity strongly emphasises algorithmic thinking and evaluation skills

What Can You Build?

- Children use six bricks to build any creature
- They then take it in turns to describe their creature

This simple activity helps develop student's creativity and can fit in with any existing theme or subject within the school. There is some opportunity to consider abstraction here.

Build a Cube

Build a cube with six bricks

This is a logical puzzle that will require logical reasoning to solve the problem. The students will be constantly evaluating their outcome and the activity can be extended to see:

- Who can do it in the fastest time?
- How to write an algorithm to create the cube

Computing Programmes of Study Statements covered by this activity:

- Computational thinking makes up the overarching purpose and aims of the computing programmes of study
- 1.1: understand what algorithms are
- 1.2: create and debug simple algorithms
- 1.3: use logical reasoning to predict the behaviour of simple programs
- 2.1: design, write and debug programs that accomplish specific goals

- 2.3: use sequence, selection, and repetition in programs
- 3.1: design, use and evaluate computational abstractions
- 3.2: understand several key algorithms that reflect computational thinking

Refer to Chapter 8 for the fully referenced Computing Programmes of Study

Jazzy Jigsaw Puzzles

Age group
Suitable for all ages

Resources required

- At least one jigsaw puzzle per learner (sample below)
- Ideally multiple jigsaw puzzles for learners to progress onto

Note

Additional puzzle sets (and puzzle artwork) can be downloaded from: www.digitalschoolhouse.org.uk/documents/jazzy-jigsaws

An online jigsaw puzzle maker is available at: www.dailyjigsawpuzzles.net/puzzle-maker.html

Introduction

Ever wondered how puzzle sets consisting of thousands of pieces are ever solved? All those pieces, mixed together, take them out of the box and what's the first thing you do?

Most people will make some attempt to begin to sort the pieces and assign some sort of order to the jumble that came tumbling out of the box. Jigsaw puzzles are well known to help develop strategic thinking and logical reasoning. What's less well known is that they also help develop computational thinking in a really fun way.

This simple classroom activity is one that can last for 5 minutes or 50 and is suitable for all age groups. Developed in collaboration with Code Kingdoms, Jazzy Jigsaws brings endless fun into any lesson or training event. Make your own Jazzy Jigsaw and switch the image with one that is more relevant for specific subjects, and hey presto it now supports cross-curricular teaching too!

Some Jazzy Computational Thinking links

Algorithmic thinking – people who solve jigsaw puzzles regularly may often devise their own strategies for solving puzzles quickly. For example, consider the strategy (algorithm) below:

1. Find the edge and corner pieces
2. Place the corner pieces
3. Sort the pieces to find the edges
4. Join the corners by placing the edge pieces (to create a frame)
5. Find pieces with a similar pattern and/or colour and group together
6. Place and fit similar pieces together
7. Arrange groups of puzzle pieces within the frame
8. Complete the puzzle by adding in the missing pieces

Decomposition – taking a large image and breaking it down. Or solving the entire puzzle by resolving smaller groups of it first. Chunking up a problem into smaller more manageable chunks is an effective way to solve a problem. We often find that we do this in jigsaw puzzles, by solving smaller parts of the puzzle first and then collectively putting them together to form the whole. (*Note: this will be easier to see of puzzles with larger pieces*)

Abstraction – the completed puzzle forms an image, a model/representation of something and can hide the complexity of all the separate pieces required to fit together to complete it.

Generalisation – if we arrive at one strategy to solve a single puzzle quickly and effectively, will the same strategy work for other jigsaw puzzles or will we need to make adjustments to our algorithm to accommodate multiple puzzle sets?

Evaluation – testing out our strategies for solving puzzles and improving them along the way.

Activity plan

Task Outline	Computational Thinking
Organise the class into pairs	
Give each pair a puzzle pack	
Set the challenge – who can solve the puzzle the fastest? Difficulty options: • show them the final image that they should be creating (*easier*) • keep the final image being made a secret (*recommended*) • allow 'sneak peaks' at the final image (*mid-way*) Hiding the final image may result in different pairs of pupils arriving at a slightly different solution. Having this result would be a good way to highlight the importance of algorithms needing to be specific. If you have a range of puzzle sets to be solved, you may want to vary the approach between them. Why is it easier if you know what you are making? If you can't see the what the final outcome is supposed to be then what strategies do you rely on to solve the puzzle? Or are different to what you would have done if you'd known what the final result is? You could choose to divide the class in half (one knows the final outcome and the other doesn't) to examine if different approaches are used.	Algorithmic thinking Decomposition
Discuss with the class: • How did you solve the puzzle? • Did you have a plan? • What did you do and why? • Do you use the same strategy to solve all your puzzles? • Did you have the same strategy as your friends?	
Let's turn this into an algorithm…pupils write their strategy as a series of instructions to solve puzzles	Algorithmic Thinking

Now test the algorithm on a new puzzle set	Evaluation, Generalisation
Discuss with the class: • Did your strategy work? • Did you need to change anything? • Compare your puzzle with the rest, have you all recreated the same image? • If there are differences, then why do these differences exist?	Evaluation
Write a plan/strategy/instructions to completing this new puzzle set specifically	Algorithmic Thinking
Swap your algorithm with another pair and test each other's algorithms. Solve the same puzzle using someone else's algorithm.	Evaluation
Discuss with the class: • Do they work? • Compare results – how can you make the instructions better?	Evaluation
Give each pair a brand new puzzle set with a different image	
Before pupils begin solving the puzzle ask them to look at the pieces. Consider and discuss: • Will the same algorithm work that you adopted last time? • Do you want to change your algorithm specifically for this puzzle pack?	Generalisation Algorithmic Thinking
Pupils solve the puzzle to help test and refine their algorithms	Algorithmic Thinking
Discuss with the class: • How good were your algorithms? • What changes did you have to make from one puzzle set to the next?	Evaluation Generalisation
Class challenge – each pair uses their refined algorithm to solve a brand new puzzle set against the clock – record the time – who wins?	
Discuss with the class: • Who won the challenge? • Which teams took the longest? • Compare the algorithms – what is different? • Why did different algorithms solve the same problems at different times? • Which algorithms were better overall and why?	Evaluation

Adding More Jazz (Extended Activities!)

Giant Class Jigsaw

Try a giant jigsaw puzzle put together by the entire class to demonstrate decomposition and create a fantastic classroom display. Prepare a giant jigsaw puzzle consisting of larger sized pieces. Templates can be downloaded or floor puzzles could be bought for the occasion.

When choosing the image for the puzzle it's better to choose a puzzle that can be broken down into distinct sections or parts; such as this giant floor puzzle: bit.ly/JigsawSample1 or this 3D construction: bit.ly/JigsawSample2.

Divide the class into teams and then encourage the students to come up with an effective strategy for sorting the puzzle pieces. The main aim is that each team ends up with a set of pieces that will enable them to collectively construct part of the puzzle. Once the teams are done, they can bring their sections together to construct the whole puzzle.

Class discussion and questioning will be invaluable here to ensure that students understand what they are doing and the importance of it. For example,

When dividing the pieces between the teams, did they employ a special strategy? What did they consider?

Did they sort the pieces at all? If so, was this done before or after dividing it into teams? Would it have been better the other way around? How did they sort the pieces? What did they look for and consider?

When bringing the different sections together, the teams will need to ensure that they are joining the correct sections together. Which bit goes where? How will they identify this, do the teams/ class have a plan for this? What criteria are they using to compare the different sections and identify the correct parts?

When integrating the separate sections together do they correctly construct the whole? This is an example of 'integration testing' strategies.

Going digital

www.dailyjigsawpuzzles.net/puzzle-maker.html is one example of an online puzzle maker that allows you to upload your own images and convert them into puzzles. Using the images downloaded as part of this activity, an alternative way to carry out the tasks set could be to use the online puzzle maker instead of physical puzzles.

However, the puzzle maker can also serve a different purpose. Once students have had a chance to explore the physical puzzles, tell them to have a go at the puzzle maker. The class can examine the online jigsaw puzzle, perhaps divide them into groups with each member of the group looking at a different website. The team mates can then come together to compare common and differing features of each jigsaw puzzle website. Using what they have learnt and through class discussion the students can then consider the key elements of the online jigsaw puzzle; for example:

- The individual pieces – each piece is a separate object
- The user can click and drag the pieces into different positions
- The pieces become fixed when placed correctly

Students can then go through a design process to eventually create their own puzzle maker in an environment such as Scratch. Although it is recommended that before students begin designing their own, their first step in the process is to explore existing solutions, which can be found here: scratch.mit.edu/search/projects?q=jigsaw+puzzle. They can then use the information gleaned from here to devise their own interactive jigsaw puzzle.

Computing Programmes of Study Statements covered by this activity:

- Computational thinking makes up the overarching purpose and aims of the computing programmes of study
- 1.1: understand what algorithms are
- 1.2: create and debug simple algorithms
- 1.3: use logical reasoning to predict the behaviour of simple programs
- 2.1: design, write and debug programs that accomplish specific goals
- 2.2: use sequence, selection, and repetition in programs; work with variables and various forms of input and output
- 2.3: use sequence, selection, and repetition in programs
- 3.1: design, use and evaluate computational abstractions
- 3.2: understand several key algorithms that reflect computational thinking
- 3.3: use two or more programming languages ... to solve a variety of computational problems

Refer to Chapter 8 for the fully referenced Computing Programmes of Study

Cat On Yer Head

Age group
Suitable for all ages

Resources required
- A crowd of at least 20 people

- Props of your own choosing if you want them

- Book and free samples can be downloaded from www. catonyerhead.com

An associated slide deck has been created by the Digital Schoolhouse and is available for download from: www.digitalschoolhouse.org. uk/documents/cat-yer-head-crowd-game

Cat On Yer Head (catonyerhead.com) is a crowd game that aims to teach key games design principles using unplugged techniques. It was originally developed by Playniac and the guidance written here has been reproduced from the work of the Digital Schoolhouse.

Why play the game?
As well as teaching the principles of Games Design, Cat on Yer Head inspires pupils to be creative. Through an iterative development process pupils 'become' the game and through peer collaboration continue to improve their game. It is this peer collaboration that is an essential part of not just developing the game, but also playing it that brings out a deeper sense of unity, allowing pupils to collectively be a part of something larger. The activity works brilliantly as an ice breaker for any session or for team bonding skills. It can be used as a lesson starter, a fun thing to do during a school assembly or something to do as part of team building sessions. The game itself also helps to develop logical reasoning, algorithmic thinking and decomposition as well as other key computational thinking skills. It's a game with built in flexibility, the games mediator through questioning can take the

game into any direction they choose and in doing so can develop links with any curriculum subject area.

Game rules

1. Ensure everyone in the group is standing/sitting within arm's reach of each other.
2. One player starts with the cat on their head and on the other side of the room another player starts with a mouse on their head.
3. The player with the cat repeats the word "cat" loudly. The cat moves when the player passes it on by tapping the shoulder of their neighbour. The next player now repeats "cat" loudly.
4. The mouse moves in the same way.
5. Cat & mouse can both move in any direction.
6. If the cat catches the mouse before the time runs out, then the cat wins. Otherwise if the mouse survives, then the mouse has won!

Playing the game – Getting Started

It is usually best if you launch into the game without too much prior explanation. Allow time to go through the simple game play instructions.

Play the first round with the original rules. Who won? Engage pupils in discussion around what happened during the game. You may want to ask the following questions:

Was it a fair game? Encourage pupils to explain and justify their answer.

How could the game be adapted? Encourage pupils to suggest their own modifications to the game.

Choose to implement one or two of the pupils' suggestions and play another round. If pupils are struggling to come up with their own ideas, then use some of the ideas from the book. For example, increasing the time, or making the mouse hunt for cheese as well as avoiding the cat. After each round have a quick discussion to encourage pupils to develop their game further. Use your questioning to help tease out the key principles of game design. For example, you may wish to ask:

- How does the game end?
- What if we changed the rules to end the game?
- How would that affect the game?
- What new rules could we develop that determined the end of the game?
- Is it fair that the cat only has to catch the mouse?
- Could we give the cat an additional goal?
- Could we build anything to give the cat benefits or rewards?
- What if there were three game characters or more?
- A cat, a mouse, and a ...?

Play multiple rounds, and in between each one use your questioning techniques to help the pupils develop the game further.

The game can continue for as long as you wish. Use it as quick 5-minute starter, or a much longer activity.

Extended activities

- A general discussion, what did pupils learn from this?
- Asking learners to jot down their ideas for their own game. Using Cat On Yer Head as a mechanism for developing their own game is a fantastic idea. Learners can play the game initially to spark off ideas, then once they have developed a game idea they can test its gameplay using the same method. Calling the class together and allowing the learners to become the game mediators to test their own game ideas is a good way

to facilitate effective collaborative working, enabling learners to visualise their creative ideas and test whether or not they would work before they put them into action.

- A more detailed discussion around game design principles and what makes a good game.

- Develop algorithmic thinking by producing a storyboard for the game they have played.

- Creative Writing/Literacy – learners can draft a story based around the game. This can be straight forward where learners write up the game they have played as a story, or it can be extended further by asking learners to first write out a story and then see if they can 'play' it out using this technique.

Computing Programmes of Study Statements covered by this activity:

Computational Thinking including its components is highlighted in the purpose of the programmes of study and is part of the overarching aims of the computing curriculum which seeks to ensure that all pupils: 'can understand and apply the fundamental principles and concepts of computer science, including abstraction, logic, algorithms and data representation.'

Refer to Chapter 8 for the fully referenced Computing Programmes of Study

Gamebook Computing

Interactive Fiction: Teaching Computing
and Computational Thinking through English

Age group

Suitable for all ages from Upper Key Stage 2 onwards

Resources required

- A class set of gamebooks. Free online versions are available at: www.ffproject.com
- Gamebook flowcharts – These ideally may be for the story being read and may therefore need to be created. Alternatively, you may use one of the flowcharts here.

What to do

Select a story to begin with the class. You may choose to begin reading the book with the class, explaining the rules and getting the class to make the initial decisions together. Once the tone has been set, divide the class into pairs and encourage them to continue reading part of the story together for a while.

Bring together three different pairs of groups to form a larger group. Each pair should describe the path their story took and compare journeys. It is likely that their stories differed, encourage them to consider how and why this was the case. What decisions made their paths differ?

It is good at this point to bring the class or groups together for a larger discussion to draw out the following ideas:

- What is the difference between a regular fiction book and a gamebook?
- Different pairs had different outcomes for the same story. This was a result of the decisions taken by each pair at each point in the story.

- Were there any instances where people made different decisions yet arrived at the same outcome? If so, how or why did that happen?
- Encourage several different groups to first consider and then contribute what they think might happen next in the story

What if we wanted a person to follow the same path in the story as us? What would be the best way to make that happen? Encourage groups to spend 10 minutes or so brainstorming and trying out different ideas. How are books like this made? Ask the students to consider how they would go about writing a book like this.

Explain that the development of the book requires the author to break down each minute element of the story into different parts (**Decomposition**). Each part will need to be considered separately, and multiple subsequent pathways considered for each element. It can be hard to keep track of this so flowcharts are often used (**Algorithmic Thinking**). The images provided with this resource show small graphic sections of the flowcharts produced by Ian Livingstone when he was writing *Armies of Death* and *Trial of Champions*. If these books are available to you, it would be a good idea to give students the opportunity to follow the story using the flowchart and comparing the two together, looking at the alternative pathways. Can they track the choices of their group using the flowchart?

If a different *Fighting Fantasy* gamebook has been used and a flowchart for it is not available, then after students have had the opportunity to look at and discuss the examples provided with this resource, encourage them to read and make their choices through the adventure, and create their own flowchart at the same time. The three different pairs in the group should come together to begin to plot the story and the alternative pathways together onto a single flowchart, comparing their choices and giving reasons for their choices. The goal is to find the optimum route through the gamebook that leads to success.

For example, for the story *Bloodsworth Bayou* by Cian Gill (free online interactive gamebook published by the fansite FF Project is available at: www.ffproject.com/bayou.htm) the flowchart may look something like the following:

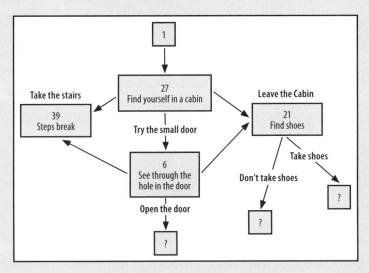

Putting the story to one side, encourage students to consider what may happen next. Each group of students should consider the flowcharts they have developed for their story so far and consider suggestions of what may happen next in the story. The group should build upon their existing flowchart and ensure that they consider all elements of the story to come next.

Note: the number assigned to each part of the story is a random assignment, designed to ensure that the next part of the story doesn't simply appear next to the one currently being read.

End the activity with each group presenting their own continuation of the story to the class.

Extended activities

Once students have become familiar with adapting and extending an existing story they can develop their own. In groups/pairs students should generate story ideas and decide on a narrative and draft outline. Together they should draw up a flowchart outlining their story.

- **Extending the work with English Lessons:** It would be useful to follow this up with work in English lessons, where students can then write each element of their story, thereby constructing and writing their own gamebook.

- **Extending the work with programming:** Encourage students to develop and test their own program, possibly using a language such as Scratch or Python, which converts their story into a digital interactive version. A web based version can also be developed by using HTML and CSS script to collate the different elements together. More advanced students will be able to use appropriate script to code additional interactive features that can keep track of common gamebook attributes such as Skill, Stamina and Luck.

- **Extending the work with Digital Literacy:** For a non-programming focus the story can be presented in multiple environments, from using the interactive features in PowerPoint, to creating an interactive flash animation or alternatively creating audio/video files to support the delivery and presentation of the story.

- **Extending the work with Art Lessons:** Whether students are presenting their final story as a coded solution or by simply developing a PDF eBook they will need accompanying artwork to help bring the story to life. A well designed book cover is an important selling point for any book. Students may design the book cover, game characters, story scenes and other graphical assets to support the presentation of their story and help bring it to life.

There is great potential for extending this work further with students producing their own eBooks which are then made publicly available for their peers to download and read.

Possible Story Ideas (for students to use)

- Maisie has just started her first day at her new secondary school. Help her make the right decisions and help her settle in and make lots of new friends

- Nita enjoys downloading music, films and games to use on her home computer. The only problem is that she doesn't pay for them. What happens when she gets caught?

- Jack loves playing games online with his friends. One day he receives a friend request from someone he's never met. What happens next?

Links with Computational Thinking

A great deal of logical reasoning is required not just to construct a gamebook story but also to follow one through. The fact that the gamebook can be easily represented with a flowchart, which can then be modified and further developed, brings in algorithmic thinking. The flowchart also demonstrates how the overall story is broken down into smaller sections which are each then dealt with separately. This demonstrates decomposition, while the overall story itself may be an abstraction of a real-life scenario. Evaluation techniques will come into play as students review and refine their stories.

Links with the Computing Programmes of Study

The core activity helps develop computational thinking and problem-solving which are part of the purpose and aims behind the curriculum. If the work is extended further then activity has the potential to easily meet the statements defined at each key stage for programming, developing creative solutions and possibly e-safety.

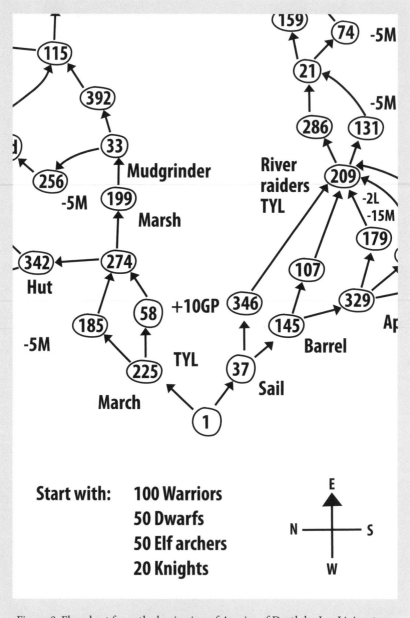

Figure 9: Flowchart from the beginning of Armies of Death by Ian Livingstone

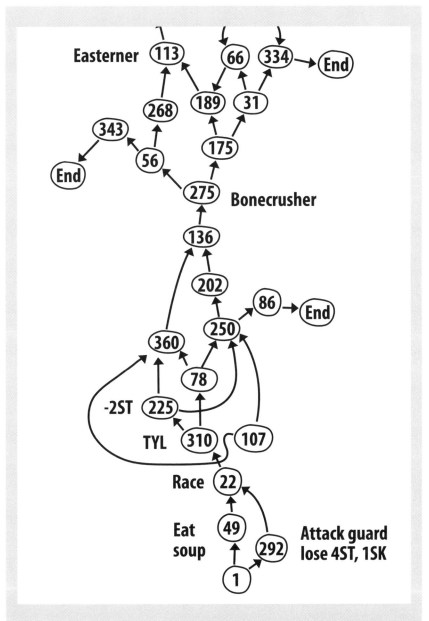

Figure 10: Flowchart from the beginning of Trial of Champions by Ian Livingstone

Computing Programmes of Study Statements covered by this activity:

Computational thinking makes up the overarching purpose and aims of the computing programmes of study

- 2.1: design, write and debug programs that accomplish specific goals
- 2.2: use sequence, selection, and repetition in programs; work with variables and various forms of input and output
- 2.3: use logical reasoning to explain how simple algorithms work...
- 2.6: select, use and combine a variety of software on a range of digital devices to design and create...
- 3.1: design, use and evaluate computational abstractions
- 3.3: use two or more programming languages ... to solve a variety of computational problems
- 3.4: understand simple Boolean logic...
- 3.7: undertake creative projects...
- 3.8: create, re-use, revise and re-purpose digital artefacts for a given audience...

Refer to Chapter 8 for the fully referenced Computing Programmes of Study

Recommended resources

Full sets of worksheets, teacher guidance notes and resources can be downloaded for all activities in this book from www.digitalschoolhouse.org.uk

Other recommended resources are:

Resource	URL	Description
Animate Competition	animation16.cs.manchester.ac.uk	Annual Computer animation competition
Apps for Good	www.appsforgood.org	Extra curricular schools programme to develop STEM, entreperneurship and design skills amongst students
BAFTA Young Games Designers Competition	ygd.bafta.org	Resource bank and portal for BAFTA's annual Young Games Designers Competition
Barefoot Computing	barefootcas.org.uk	A CPD programme & resource bank focusing on computer science concepts for primary age pupils
Big Bang Legends	www.bigbanglegends.com	Ready to fight antimatter monsters? Say what? Exactly! A mix of particle physics and full blown action game. Learning has never been so fun! Lightneer aim to make learning games, which are as fun as they are educational. Their first game Big Bang Legends aims to teach particle physics.
CAS Computational Thinking Framework	community.computingatschool.org.uk/resources/2324	CAS Computational Thinking – A guide for teachers to help develop an understanding of computational thinking in practice
CAS QuickStart Computing	www.quickstartcomputing.org	A CPD toolkit to help deliver inspirational computing lessons
Code Club	www.codeclub.org.uk	Nationwide network of volunteer led school coding clubs
Coder Dojo	coderdojo.com	A worldwide movement of free, volunteer-led, community-based programming clubs for young people
Code Kingdoms	codekingdoms.com	Unique editor to help students learn to code through Minecraft
Code.org	code.org	Initiative to improve access to computing for a diverse range of learners. Founders of the Hour of Code
Computing Curriculum Guide	www.computingguide.org	A guide to support senior leaders with embedding the new computing curriculum into schools

CS4FN	www.cs4fn.org	Computer Science for Fun – Exploring how computer science is fun!
Erase All Kittens	eraseallkittens.com	A story driven game to teach children computational thinking and programming concepts
GameMaker	www.yoyogames.com/gamemaker	Professional game development environment suitable for use in schools with Key Stage 3 students
Innovate My Curriculum	innovatemycurriculum.com	Planning and Assessment tool for the computing curriculum
LEGO Education	education.lego.com/en-gb	LEGO resources to help teach STEM and Computing in schools
Raspberry Pi Foundation	www.raspberrypi.org/about	Creators of the Raspberry Pi, hub for latest resources and guidance
Teaching London Computing	teachinglondoncomputing.org	Official resource website for Computing At School London Regional Centre
Tenderfoot Computing	www.computingatschool.org.uk/tenderfoot	A CPD programme covering cmputer science concepts, aimed at Key Stage 3 teachers
Unity	unity3d.com	Professional game development environment suitable for use in schools with Key Stage 4 students and above

Chapter 8

Useful Information

National Curriculum in England: Computing Programmes of Study[40]

Purpose of study

A high-quality computing education equips pupils to use computational thinking and creativity to understand and change the world. Computing has deep links with mathematics, science and design and technology, and provides insights into both natural and artificial systems. The core of computing is computer science, in which pupils are taught the principles of information and computation, how digital systems work and how to put this knowledge to use through programming. Building on this knowledge and understanding, pupils are equipped to use information technology to create programs, systems and a range of content. Computing also ensures that pupils become digitally literate – able to use, and express themselves and develop their ideas through, information and communication technology – at a level suitable for the future workplace and as active participants in a digital world.

---

40. This section has been reproduced from the original version, which can be found here: www.gov.uk/government/publications/national-curriculum-in-england-computing-programmes-of-study/. The only modifications made to the original document is the numbered referencing which has been added to each statement.

Aims

The National Curriculum for computing aims to ensure that all pupils:

- can understand and apply the fundamental principles and concepts of computer science, including abstraction, logic, algorithms and data representation
- can analyse problems in computational terms, and have repeated practical experience of writing computer programs in order to solve such problems
- can evaluate and apply information technology, including new or unfamiliar technologies, analytically to solve problems
- are responsible, competent, confident and creative users of information and communication technology

Key stage 1

1. Pupils should be taught to:

1.1. understand what algorithms are; how they are implemented as programs on digital devices; and that programs execute by following precise and unambiguous instructions

1.2. create and debug simple programs

1.3. use logical reasoning to predict the behaviour of simple programs

1.4. use technology purposefully to create, organise, store, manipulate and retrieve digital content

1.5. recognise common uses of information technology beyond school

1.6. use technology safely and respectfully, keeping personal information private; identify where to go for help and support when they have concerns about content or contact on the internet or other online technologies.

Key stage 2

2. Pupils should be taught to:

2.1. design, write and debug programs that accomplish specific goals, including controlling or simulating physical systems; solve problems by decomposing them into smaller parts

2.2. use sequence, selection, and repetition in programs; work with variables and various forms of input and output

2.3. use logical reasoning to explain how some simple algorithms work and to detect and correct errors in algorithms and programs

2.4. understand computer networks including the internet; how they can provide multiple services, such as the world wide web; and the opportunities they offer for communication and collaboration

2.5. use search technologies effectively, appreciate how results are selected and ranked, and be discerning in evaluating digital content

2.6. select, use and combine a variety of software (including internet services) on a range of digital devices to design and create a range of programs, systems and content that accomplish given goals, including collecting, analysing, evaluating and presenting data and information

2.7. use technology safely, respectfully and responsibly; recognise acceptable/unacceptable behaviour; identify a range of ways to report concerns about content and contact.

Key stage 3

3. Pupils should be taught to:

3.1. design, use and evaluate computational abstractions that model the state and behaviour of real-world problems and physical systems

3.2. understand several key algorithms that reflect computational thinking [for example, ones for sorting and searching]; use logical reasoning to compare the utility of alternative algorithms for the same problem

3.3. use two or more programming languages, at least one of which is textual, to solve a variety of computational problems; make appropriate use of data structures [for example, lists, tables or arrays]; design and develop modular programs that use procedures or functions

3.4. understand simple Boolean logic [for example, AND, OR and NOT] and some of its uses in circuits and programming; understand how numbers can be represented in binary, and be able to carry out simple operations on binary numbers [for example, binary addition, and conversion between binary and decimal]

3.5. understand the hardware and software components that make up computer systems, and how they communicate with one another and with other systems

3.6. understand how instructions are stored and executed within a computer system; understand how data of various types (including text, sounds and pictures) can be represented and manipulated digitally, in the form of binary digits

3.7. undertake creative projects that involve selecting, using, and combining multiple applications, preferably across a range of devices, to achieve challenging goals, including collecting and analysing data and meeting the needs of known users

3.8. create, re-use, revise and re-purpose digital artefacts for a given audience, with attention to trustworthiness, design and usability

3.9. understand a range of ways to use technology safely, respectfully, responsibly and securely, including protecting their online identity and privacy; recognise inappropriate content, contact and conduct and know how to report concerns.

Key stage 4

All pupils must have the opportunity to study aspects of information technology and computer science at sufficient depth to allow them to progress to higher levels of study or to a professional career.

4. All pupils should be taught to:

4.1. develop their capability, creativity and knowledge in computer science, digital media and information technology

4.2. develop and apply their analytic, problem-solving, design, and computational thinking skills

4.3. understand how changes in technology affect safety, including new ways to protect their online privacy and identity, and how to identify and report a range of concerns.

Matrix of Activities against the Computing Programmes of Study Statements

Activity	Computing Programmes of Study Statements																									
	1.1	1.2	1.3	1.4	1.5	1.6	2.1	2.2	2.3	2.4	2.5	2.6	2.7	3.1	3.2	3.3	3.4	3.5	3.6	3.7	3.8	3.9	4.1	4.2	4.3	CT
Making Faces: Playdough Programming	✓	✓	✓				✓		✓					✓	✓									✓		✓
The Guessing Game																								✓		✓
Pixel Puzzle	✓	✓	✓				✓	✓	✓					✓	✓				✓					✓		✓
Nifty Networks										✓	✓							✓								✓
The Computational Thinking Duck	✓	✓	✓				✓		✓					✓	✓									✓		✓
Jazzy Jigsaw Puzzles	✓	✓					✓	✓	✓					✓	✓	✓							✓			✓
Cat On Yer Head												✓								✓	✓		✓	✓		✓
Gamebook Computing							✓	✓	✓					✓	✓	✓	✓						✓	✓		✓

The full set of resources for each activity can be downloaded from www. digitalschoolhouse.org.uk

Glossary of key terms

Computing At School have published an online glossary of key terminology associated with the new computing curriculum at: www.teachprimarycomputing.org.uk/glossary/. For ease of use, some of the terms and definitions from this site have been reproduced here.

Terminology	Definition
Algorithm	An algorithm is a step by step process by which a desired outcome is achieved. Algorithms can be constructed using words, images, symbols, or a programming language. We all use algorithms on a daily basis, when classes line up for assembly, when we follow a cooking recipe or when build LEGO models or IKEA furniture. When creating their own algorithms, pupils need to identify what the goal is and sequence their instructions in the correct order.
Computer networks	The computers and the connecting hardware (wifi access points, cables, fibres, switches and routers) that make it possible to transfer data using an agreed method ('protocol'). Computers and wireless devices that are connected to the same server and the hardware that allows these connections (wifi access points, cables, fibres, switches routers) are part of a computer network. Theses devices are able to exchange data with each other using an agreed method ('protocol'). A small network such as one at home or at school is known as a local area network (LAN). When smaller networks join together a larger, wide area network (WAN) is formed. The biggest WAN is the internet.
Computational thinking	Computational thinking allows us to develop skills and techniques to help us solve problems effectively, with or without the aid of a computer.
Debug	When a program doesn't achieve the desired outcome it is because we have not instructed the computer correctly. The mistake we have made is referred to as a bug; the process by which the bug is located and corrected is know as debugging. A risotto recipe which instructs one to add 2 tbps of salt will not produce the delicious meal that was expected. By debugging this algorithm and replacing with 2 tsp the algorithm has been debugged and the desired outcome has been reached. We should encourage children to use logical reasoning when debugging. When programming a quiz, we might end up with a message telling us that the incorrect answer we have given is correct. This should lead us to think that the bug might be in the selection statements for that given answer.
Decomposition	Decomposition is one of the 6 key concepts of computational thinking and is concerned with breaking a problem or a system down into its parts. Pupils have plenty of experience of this in primary schools: they partition numbers when adding; they plan settings, characters and a 5 part plot before story writing, they identify materials, equipment and processes needed before making DT products. When writing more complex programs, children should be encouraged to think about the different things that their program needs to do in order to achieve its goal. A simple maze game in scratch might need: a maze; a sprite to move around the maze; the means by which to move the sprite; a timer; selection statements to define what happens if the maze wall is touched. By identifying such criteria first, children will then understand the different parts their program will need to incorporate.

Logical reasoning	Logical reasoning is one of the 6 key concepts of computational thinking and is concerned with a systematic approach to solving problems or deducing information using a set of universally applicable and totally reliable rules. The use of our experiences and understanding of a topic or concept to help solve a problem or deduce information. When decoding words children use their knowledge of phonics to deduce how a word might sound. Upon seeing the word *cinder* for the first time, a child, applying logical reasoning, would predict that the word has a soft c sound because their experience of other *ci* words. Children are expected to use their knowledge of the software or hardware they are using to help solve problems and fix errors. A child who knows that a bee-bot has to travel the long way around rather than jumping over a gap, is showing and applying their knowledge. When creating an animation in scratch, a pupil will identify the need for delays when characters are in conversation. For pupils to be able to apply logical reasoning we must give them suitable opportunities to engage with purposeful problem-solving.
Pattern recognition	In many areas of the curriculum, we ask children to identify patterns. This might be the key features of a specific author's openings, what happens when two odd numbers are added or the most common shops on a high street. Once patterns have been identified, pupils are required to use these patterns to make predictions, create solutions and develop reasoning. When creating a quiz using scratch, a child may identify and fix a common problem with the scoring systems by resetting the variable value to zero at the start of the script. When moving on to creating more complex games or using a different programming language, the child should readily identify the need to reset any variables to the initial value at the beginning of the program.
Program	A program is an algorithm that is written in (or translated to) a language that a computer understands. The computer follows these instructions precisely and therefore they need to be unambiguous. When using logo we might want the turtle to move up the screen but the command up is not one that the computer understands, so we have to use the predefined vocabulary and the correct syntax, in this case *FD 10*. Similarly when constructing a square, if we read an instruction telling us to turn right we would assume that we need to turn 90°. However a computer, a device with no intelligence, would not query this and would follow the instruction given.
Repetition	When writing programs we should encourage children to be concise. Repetition is a way to get the computer to following the same set of instructions forever, a given number of times or until a condition is met. When writing a program to create a square we can tell the computer to repeat the instruction forward 10 right 90 four times. For most of us we repeat the same get up, eat breakfast, get ready, go to work algorithm each day until the day condition *is day Saturday or Sunday?* is met. Repetition is sometimes referred to as loops or forever loops and are often combined with selection statements.
Selection	Part of a computer program that is only executed if a certain condition is met. They share a lot in common with modal verbs and conditional sentences. It is useful to think of the words if, then, else when creating unplugged selection procedures. For example, when walking through a maze trying to avoid the *Great Fire of London* pupils might use the following selection statement: **If** there is fire in front of me **then** turn around **else** carry on. When creating programs we can use variables, internal and external inputs in selection statements. For example when using a class noise monitoring system, a warning sign may appear on screen when the noise level exceeds a given threshold.

Sequence	When we create algorithms we must sequence the steps in the order they have to be followed. For example, when putting fuel in the car the fuel-tank cap has to be removed, then the nozzle inserted, before fuel is pumped into the car. If this set of instructions is sequenced in a different way we will not get the petrol into the fuel tank. Think of the puzzle whereby we need to get the farmer, the chicken, the fox and the corn across the river. If the steps are not sequenced correctly then either the corn, the chicken or both will get eaten. Pupils need to understand that digital devices follow programs blindly they will do what they have been instructed to do in the order given.
Simulation	Using a computer to model the state and behaviour of real-world (or imaginary) systems, including physical and social systems; an integral part of most computer games.

Other computing glossaries

Teach ICT: www.teach-ict.com/glossary/A.htm

BBC Web Wise: www.bbc.co.uk/webwise/a-z/

Fact Monster: www.factmonster.com/ipka/A0006024.html

Glossary, Games mechanics

Pulsipher Games Glossary: pulsiphergames.com/
glossaryforgamedesigners.pdf

What Games are: www.whatgamesare.com/glossary.html

Ian Livingstone's recommended list of proprietary video games that promote learning

Games to play as a family	Any-age single player games
Ticket to Ride	Plants Vs. Zombies
Minecraft	Snake Pass
The Legend of Zelda: Breath of the Wild	Terraria
Words with Friends	Monument Valley
Heads Up!	Tetris

The video games parents should have in the home from the age of five			
Aged 5+	*Aged 7+*	*Aged 10+*	*Aged 15+*
Cut The Rope	Minecraft	Little Big Planet	The Legend of Zelda: Breath of the Wild
Where's My Water?	Animal Crossing	Scribblenauts	Rollercoaster Tycoon
Big Bang Legends	Big Bang Legends	Lego: Star Wars	Football Manager
		The Legend of Zelda: Breath of the Wild	Civilization
			Sim City